Moodle 1.9 Math

Integrate interactive math presentations, incorporate Flash games, build feature-rich quizzes, set online tests, and monitor student progress using the Moodle e-learning platform

Ian Wild

PUBLISHING

BIRMINGHAM - MUMBAI

D1473188

Moodle 1.9 Math

First published: November 2009

Production Reference: 1181109

Published by Packt Publishing Ltd.
32 Lincoln Road
Olton
Birmingham, B27 6PA, UK.

ISBN 978-1-847196-44-6

www.packtpub.com

Cover Image by Parag Kadam (paragvkadam@gmail.com)

Credits

Author
Ian Wild

Reviewers
Mary Cooch

Mauno Korpelainen

Howard Miller

Acquisition Editor
David Barnes

Development Editor
Darshana Shinde

Technical Editor
Bhupali Khule

Indexers
Monica Ajmera

Hemangini Bari

Editorial Team Leader
Akshara Aware

Project Team Leader
Lata Basantani

Project Coordinator
Rajashree Hamine

Proofreader
Jade Schuler

Production Coordinator
Dolly Dasilva

Cover Work
Dolly Dasilva

About the Author

Ian Wild, a physicist by profession, has always focused primarily on communication and learning.

Fifteen years spent in private industry designing communication systems software eventually saw Ian concentrate on the development of accessibility and learning aids for blind, partially sighted, dyslexic, and dyscalculic computer users, while also working part-time as a math and science tutor

Teaching only part-time meant not spending as much time with his students as he would have wanted. This, and his background in learning and communication technology, seeded his interest in virtual learning environments.

Ian is author of the popular book *Moodle Course Conversion: Beginner's Guide* also from Packt Publishing.

He lives in rural Worcestershire with his wife Karen and three children Matthew, Lian, and Ethan. To learn more about Ian and his work, visit `http://www.yourmathstutor.info`.

Acknowledgements

The one aspect I enjoy most about being an author is having the opportunity to work with wonderful people. Firstly, I must thank the development and editorial teams at Packt Publishing, most notably David Barnes, Rajashree Hamine, Darshana Shinde, and Bhupali Khule. Thank you for your wisdom, guidance and, above all, your patience. A thank you must go to the reviewers for keeping my work focused and on track. Their input has been invaluable. I must thank you, the reader, for taking the time to read this book. I do hope you find it useful. I will mention quickly that if you do need any further help at all with mathematics support in Moodle, then please do visit the Mathematics Tools forum on **Moodle.org** (`http://moodle.org/mod/forum/view.php?id=752`). That's where you'll find me and my colleagues, all ready to help you with your Moodle math-related issues.

My final and very big thank you must, of course, go to Martin Dougiamas and his team. Please keep up the excellent work.

About the Reviewers

Mary Cooch is the author of *Moodle 1.9 for Teaching 7-14 Year Olds* from Packt Publishing and has taught languages and geography in the UK for over 20 years. She manages several websites, even more Moodles, and runs her own Moodle blog. A Moodle Certified Course Creator, she now spends part of her working week traveling the country as a VLE trainer specializing in Moodle. She regularly promotes its benefits in schools and has a deep understanding of what works best for younger students. Known online as moodlefairy, Mary helps moderate the forums on www.moodle.org where she aims to enthuse others with her passion for this Open Source Virtual Learning Environment.

Mary works at Our Lady's Catholic High School in Preston Lancashire UK, and can be contacted on mco@olchs.lancs.sch.uk.

> I would like to express my thanks to my family for their patience and to Our Lady's Preston Assistant Headteacher, Mark Greenwood, for his unique motivation.

Mauno Korpelainen teaches Mathematics for high school and adult students in Hyvinkää, Finland and has been several years a PHM (Particularly Helpful Moodler) and moderator of Mathematics Tools forum on **Moodle.org**.

To my family with love

Table of Contents

Preface

You've started converting your mathematics teaching over to Moodle. Perhaps you've been reading the general guides to teaching with Moodle: *Moodle Course Conversion* (ISBN: 1847195245), *Moodle 1.9 for Teaching 7-14 Year Olds* (ISBN: 1847197140), or *Moodle 1.9 E-Learning Course Development* (ISBN: 1847193536). However, teaching mathematics online means we have special requirements when it comes to how we present information to our students.

The most obvious is mathematical notation. How do we insert a simple fraction into a Moodle web page? What about derivatives, integrals, or matrices? In this book, you'll find simple and effective solutions to the problem of including mathematical notation in your Moodle courses.

Then, there's how we present data to our students; how do we quickly and easily include graphs and charts in a Moodle course? We will see more samples and solutions that you can use in your teaching.

And what's great about moving over to Moodle is that we can set online tests and have the computer mark them for us. In this book, we'll be showing you how to create math-specific questions—including how to configure Moodle so that it can recognize that $3x+4$ is algebraically equivalent to $4+3x$.

What's great about being a teacher of math is that there is a wealth of engaging and entertaining teaching material available for us to include in our Moodle courses. This book shows you the most efficient and effective ways of including a variety of content—from interactive math exploration tools to online simulations—with minimum fuss.

Because of the specialized nature of math teaching, we are required to assume some familiarity with Moodle. Otherwise, this book would have been twice as long! If you are completely new to Moodle then visit `http://www.packtpub.com/moodle-books`, and check out the other great Moodle books from Packt Publishing, especially the Beginner's Guide series.

Above all, the focus of this book is on getting results fast, moving your mathematics teaching over to Moodle so that your lessons become more effective for students and less work for you.

What this book covers

Chapter 1: Moodle Mathematics explains how to upload past exam papers for students themselves to access through the Internet. You will learn how to include a forum so that students can discuss problems they are having and where we teachers can gauge the areas we need to go over again in class. In my case, students were having problems with the Pythagorean Theorem, so I'm going to create an online Pythagorean Theorem course in Moodle.

Chapter 2: Getting Started with Mathematical Notation shows you how to include mathematical notation in your Moodle courses using the tools you will be familiar with: Microsoft Office and OpenOffice.org. You will also learn how Moodle's built-in Algebra Filter can be used to create simple mathematical notation.

Chapter 3: Enhancing your Math Teaching teaches you how to create an interactive PowerPoint presentation and shows you the different ways of incorporating presentations in a Moodle course. There are many great math videos on YouTube, and you'll learn how to include those videos in a Moodle course.

Chapter 4: SCORM and Flash discusses how to include SCORM and Flash resources in your Moodle courses. SCORM and Flash are two formats that are becoming more popular with content providers (who know that SCORM and Flash resources will work in any VLE).

Chapter 5: Geometry introduces a powerful, free tool that we can use to create interactive geometry tasks for our students. It's called GeoGebra, and this is the application that we'll be concentrating on in this chapter. What's great about GeoGebra is that there's also a Moodle filter available that allows us to embed GeoGebra activities in our Moodle courses.

Chapter 6: Math Quizzes provides solutions for teachers who are tired of marking all of those math tests. Now, we can have Moodle do all of the grading for us! In this chapter, you'll see that the Moodle Quiz module not only automatically marks the answers for us, but it also copes with different units (for example, answers given in feet or inches, meters or centimeters). You'll also learn how to enhance Moodle to recognize answers that are algebraically equivalent.

Chapter 7: More Mathematical Notation investigates three additional filters, which you can use to generate more complex mathematical notation: TeX, jsMath, and ASCIIMathML.

Chapter 8: Graphs and Charts shows you how to include graphs and charts in your Moodle course. ASCIIMathML (introduced in Chapter 7) includes a powerful component that allows us to easily incorporate graphs of functions in our Moodle courses. We will also be learning how to create charts in Microsoft Office, OpenOffice.org, and Google Docs, and we will learn the best ways of including these in our courses.

Chapter 9: Doing More with Math and Science brings all of our work in the previous eight chapters together. We investigate more methods of creating mathematical notation (including scientific notation) and learn how to include teaching resources (other than SCORM and Flash) in our Moodle courses. We end the chapter by learning how to install Jmol, a 3D interactive molecule viewer.

What you need for this book

This book is aimed at educators but, because of the specialized nature of mathematics teaching, some of the examples we give in this book require third-party tools to be installed in your Moodle. If you do need to install any new software components, then you will need access to the server Moodle is running on and permission to make changes. If you need more information on Moodle administration then check out *Moodle Administration* (ISBN: 1847195628), also available from Packt Publishing (see `http://www.packtpub.com/moodle-administration-guide/book` for details).

Who this book is for

If you are a teacher, lecturer, or trainer faced with incorporating mathematical content into a Moodle course, then this book is for you. You may want to include mathematical or scientific notation or a graph or chart. You'll learn how to do this, and more, in this book. This book assumes you are familiar with a Moodle course and with Moodle terminology. If you are completely new to Moodle, then we suggest you check out the Beginner's Guide series, also from Packt Publishing: *Moodle Course Conversion* (ISBN: 1847195245) and *Moodle 1.9 for Teaching 7-14 Year Olds* (ISBN: 1847197140).

If you are a Moodle administrator and you need your Moodle to support mathematics or science teaching, then this book will give you the instructions necessary to install all of the critical tools and enhancements your teaching colleagues will require.

Conventions

In this book, you will find a number of styles of text that distinguish between different kinds of information. Here are some examples of these styles and an explanation of their meaning.

New terms and **important words** are shown in bold. Words that you see on the screen, in menus or dialog boxes for example, appear in our text like this: "Scroll down to the **Other settings** block and choose the **Grading method** from the drop-down menu."

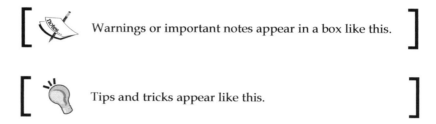

Warnings or important notes appear in a box like this.

Tips and tricks appear like this.

Reader feedback

Feedback from our readers is always welcome. Let us know what you think about this book—what you liked or may have disliked. Reader feedback is important for us to develop titles that you really get the most out of.

To send us general feedback, simply drop an email to feedback@packtpub.com, and mention the book title in the subject of your message.

If there is a book that you need and would like to see us publish, please send us a note in the **SUGGEST A TITLE** form on www.packtpub.com or email suggest@packtpub.com.

If there is a topic that you have expertise in and you are interested in either writing or contributing to a book, see our author guide at www.packtpub.com/authors.

Customer support

Now that you are the proud owner of a Packt Publishing book, we have a number of things to help you to get the most from your purchase.

Errata

Although we have taken every care to ensure the accuracy of our contents, mistakes do happen. If you find a mistake in one of our books—maybe a mistake in text or code—we would be grateful if you would report this to us. By doing so, you can save other readers from frustration and help us to improve subsequent versions of this book. If you find any errata, please report them by visiting http://www.packtpub.com/support, selecting your book, clicking on the **let us know** link, and entering the details of your errata. Once your errata are verified, your submission will be accepted and the errata added to any list of existing errata. Any existing errata can be viewed by selecting your title from http://www.packtpub.com/support.

Piracy

Piracy of copyright material on the Internet is an ongoing problem across all media. At Packt Publishing, we take the protection of our copyright and licenses very seriously. If you come across any illegal copies of our works in any form on the Internet, please provide us with the location address or web site name immediately so that we can pursue a remedy.

Please contact us at copyright@packtpub.com with a link to the suspected pirated material.

We appreciate your help in protecting our authors and our ability to bring you valuable content.

Questions

You can contact us at questions@packtpub.com if you are having a problem with any aspect of the book, and we will do our best to address it.

1
Moodle Mathematics

You are getting to grips with converting your mathematics teaching over to Moodle. Suppose you want to include a fragment of mathematics notation in your course. It might be a simple fraction, say $\frac{1}{2}$. Many will simply write this as 1/2, using a forward slash between the '1' and the '2'. However, writing fractions in this notation often causes confusion and looks slightly unprofessional. To overcome this, you would rather have a nice horizontal vinculum between the numerator and denominator. The need to write a fraction properly is a simple requirement, and one that's obviously not limited to purely mathematics teaching, or even to a numerate discipline. But what if you need to include a much more complex fragment of mathematics, such as the continuous compounding of interest in economics:

$$P \times (\lim_{m \to \infty}(1 + \frac{r}{m})^{mt})$$

What is the best way to include mathematical notation in a Moodle course? What if you don't want to stop at just mathematical notation? For instance, how do you include graphs of functions? What free tools are available to support teaching different branches of mathematics (for example, geometry) in Moodle? If it isn't obvious, how to include something as trivial as a fraction in a Moodle course, then is it going to be difficult to include something more complicated? You'll find the answers to these questions (and many more) in this book.

We'll start this chapter by exploring the advantages of converting mathematics teaching over to Moodle. Then, I'm going to begin converting my teaching over to Moodle by uploading a past exam paper to my new Moodle course. In order to support my students as they work through the paper and to judge what subject areas we need to go over again before the actual exam, I'm going to provide an online discussion area.

In this chapter we will do the following:

- Explore the advantages of converting mathematics teaching over to Moodle
- Learn how to upload a past exam paper to your Moodle course
- See how easy it is to include an online discussion area in your course

Concepts that are generally hard to visualize (geometry, for example) can be explored interactively (we'll be looking at just a few examples of how this can be achieved in this book). Complex mathematical processes can be explored and investigated at your own pace, and explanations of mathematical processes can be repeated as many times as you need (for example, in a video tutorial). Do you teach blind or visually impaired students? If implemented correctly, moving mathematics teaching online to Moodle can make the notation far more accessible. We'll see how in the later chapters.

Although I assume that you will have an admin at hand to help you set up Moodle to support mathematics, I will certainly be including detailed instructions on how to configure Moodle where that's necessary.

Are you a Moodle administrator?

In this book, you'll find detailed instructions on how to configure your Moodle site to support mathematics teaching. Mathematics teachers are a special bunch; it's fair to say that our requirements aren't very well satisfied by an out-of-the-box Moodle install. You'll want to provide the tools that allow your teaching colleagues to create fun, engaging, and innovative online mathematics courses.

In this book, we will be working together to create a Moodle course covering the Pythagorean Theorem. If you aren't teaching mathematics, but want to know how to include mathematics notation in your courses and are put off by not remembering much about Pythagoras, then please don't worry. The key issue is that we work through creating a Moodle course on a topic that will allow us to gain experience using Moodle's most beneficial mathematics tools.

What version of Moodle will I need?

This book is written for Moodle 1.9.x (in fact, I used version 1.9.5 when writing this book). I've tried to include as many screenshots as possible, but don't worry if your Moodle looks slightly different when compared to mine; Moodle can be themed (branded with your organization's logo and colors). In case you're wondering, the theme I'm using is **standardwhite**. If you do want your Moodle to look like mine, you may need to ask your Moodle admin (if that's not you!) to change the theme for you.

So, let's make a start!

Introduction to teaching Mathematics with Moodle

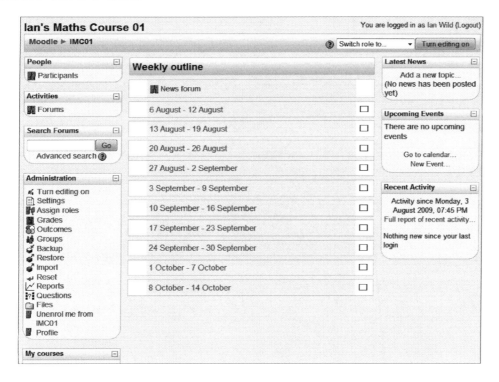

I've got plenty of worksheets, homework handouts, and old exam papers, which I've currently handed out to my students using a shared drive. The big problem I have with our shared drive is that my students always claim that they can never find the work I hand out to them (and if you've seen what a mess the shared drive is at my school, you'd be inclined to believe them).

Let's take a past exam paper and upload that to my Moodle course. First, you'll need to press the **Turn editing on** button. You'll find this in the top right-hand corner of the page:

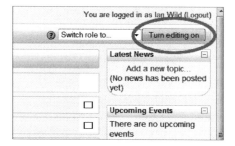

Now, I have the opportunity to add resources and activities to my course and arrange and configure the blocks on the left and right sides of the page:

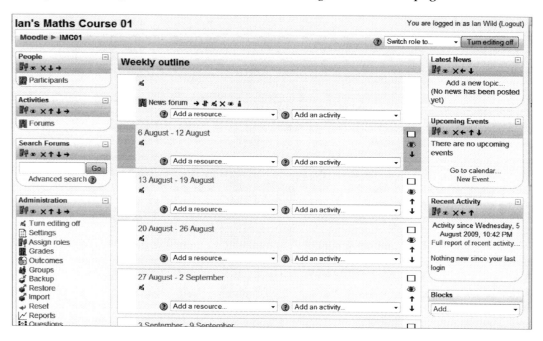

In each week, there are two drop-down menus. If you haven't already, try exploring these menus now to see what options you have:

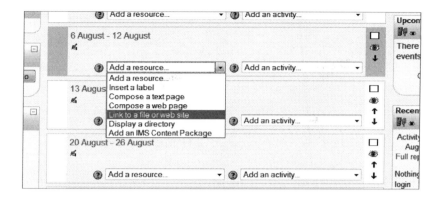

I'm going to choose the first week listed in my course. Click on the **Add a resource** drop-down menu and select **Link to a file or web site**:

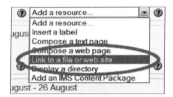

Now, I'm going to upload a file to my course as follows:

1. Clicking on the **Link to a file or web site** menu option displays the **Adding a new Resource...** page:

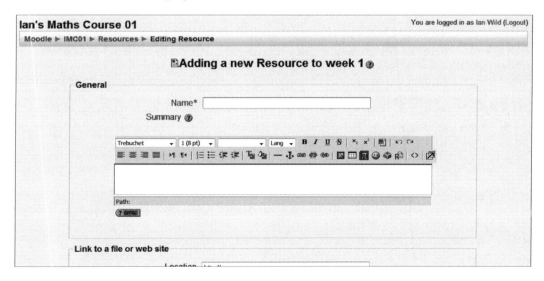

2. Give the link a **Name** and type a brief description into the **Summary** box:

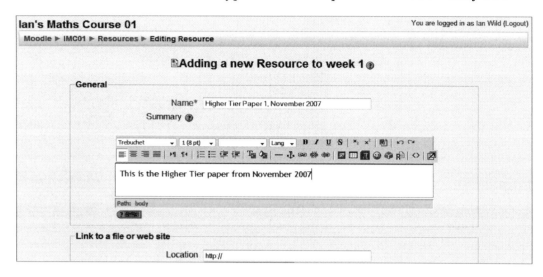

3. I'm going to upload an old exam paper, so I need to scroll down to the **Link to a file or web site** box and press the **Choose or upload a file** button:

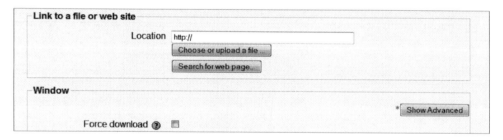

4. Each course has its own file area—a bit like **My Documents** in Windows. A new window is displayed showing the contents of the files area for this course, which is empty at the moment:

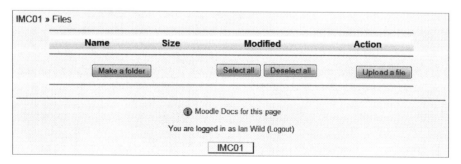

5. I need to upload the exam paper to the course files area, and to do that I first need to click on the **Upload a file** button under the **Action** heading:

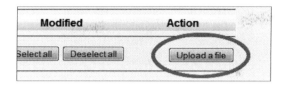

6. I'm now given the opportunity to choose a file on my computer (or from a drive on the network). Select the file you wish to upload, and click on the **Upload this file** button:

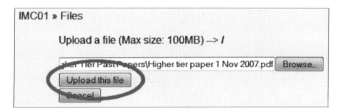

7. Now that the file is uploaded, you'll see it listed in the course files area. To select the file, you need to click on **Choose**:

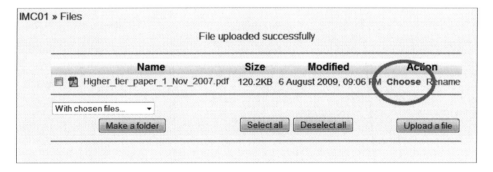

8. The name of the file will now be specified in the **Link to a file or web site** box:

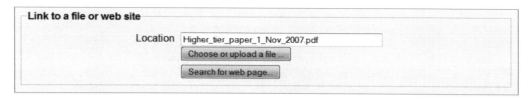

9. You now need to configure how the file is going to be displayed. I've had problems in the past with students clicking on a file in Moodle, which the browser then opens in the browser itself, making Moodle *disappear*. For now, I'm going to scroll down to the **Window** box and select **New window** from the **Window** drop-down menu (I'll speak more about how files can be displayed later in this section):

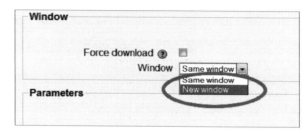

10. Scroll down to the bottom of the page and press the **Save and return to course** button:

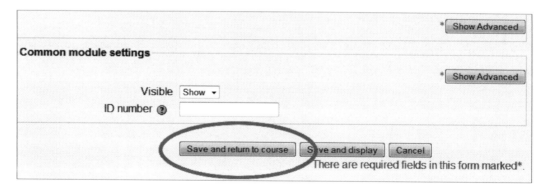

11. I now have a link to the exam paper on my course's front page:

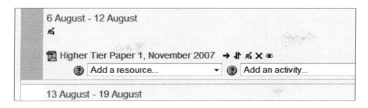

And that's all, there is to it! Try clicking on the link to make sure that the file is displayed correctly.

Before moving on, here are some hints and tips regarding file upload:

- Want to upload a lot of files all in one go? Use a compression utility and upload the ZIP file. Alternatively, in Windows, select your files and right-click on them. Slide down to the **Send To** option and choose **Compressed (zipped) Folder**. Moodle contains a built-in decompression utility. It will also remember folder structures, if you have folders within folders.

- Want to change the way a file is displayed? Rather than having the file opened in a new window, I can choose to display a navigation bar across the top of the page. I can choose that setting on the **Adding a new Resource** page. To reveal the setting, you will have to press the **Show Advanced** button in the **Window** box. Set **Window** to **Same window** and **Keep navigation visible on the same page** to **Yes, without frame**:

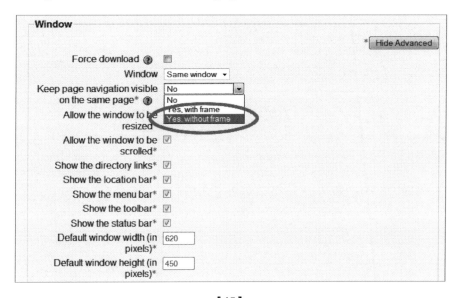

Here's how that old exam paper is now displayed:

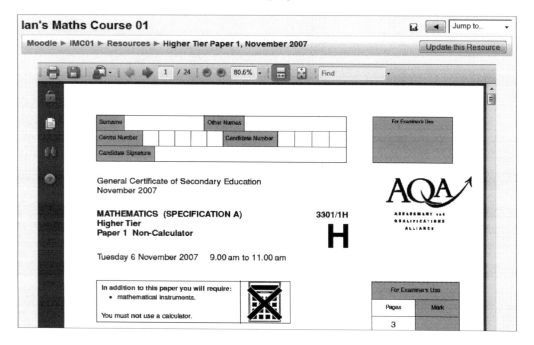

You can upload any digital file to Moodle. But remember, your students will need to have the correct software installed on their computers to view the file. If in doubt, speak to your System Administrator.

[You can manage all the files uploaded to your course by clicking on the **Files** link in the course Administration block.]

Starting an online discussion

Now, I've uploaded an old exam paper to a place where students can discuss problems they are having. This will not only allow me to monitor the topics my students are having problems with, but this will also be a place where students can help each other, encouraging collaborative learning.

What we need now is a Moodle Forum. Let's learn how you can add a forum to your course:

1. Return to your course's front page, and with editing turned on, click on the **Add an activity** drop-down menu. Choose **Forum**:

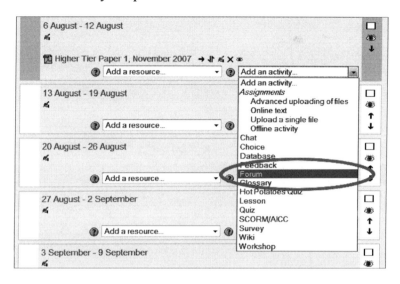

2. Give the forum a name and type in an introduction:

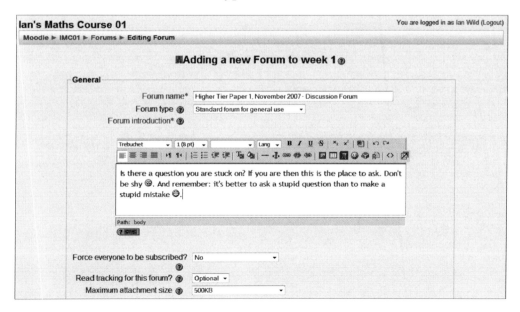

3. For a simple online discussion forum, the default settings will be fine. Scroll down to the bottom of the page and press the **Save and return to course** button:

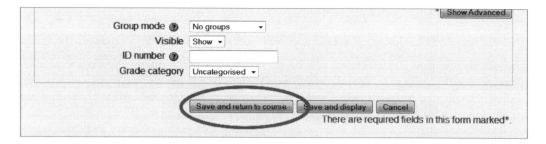

4. That's it! I'm done. I've uploaded a past paper and have a place where students can discuss questions they have about the paper:

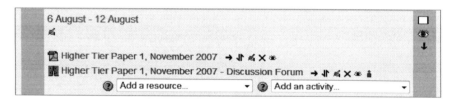

Obviously, there are a lot of settings in there that I skipped, but hopefully you can see how easy it is to create a simple discussion forum. Click on the link to the forum and experiment with making a post (don't worry, you can delete any test posts you make).

Rather than spending time discussing forums in detail, let me direct you to *Moodle Course Conversion: Beginner's Guide*. In that book, you'll find more information on forums, including forum moderation strategies.

[

Need more help with Moodle resources and activities?
In this chapter I've covered the very basics. There's plenty more information in *Moodle Course Conversion: Beginner's Guide*.
]

Configuring your course

I've uploaded a past paper in my Moodle course, and I've included a forum to allow us to discuss issues arising from that past paper online. How about exploring a couple of more important course configuration options? Again, I'm not going to go into too much detail regarding reconfiguring a course, but I will quickly direct you to three important settings.

1. Return to your course's front page and look for the **Settings** option in the course **Administration** block:

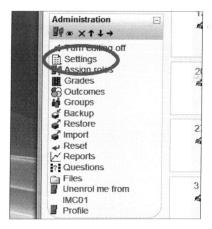

2. On the **Edit course settings** page, we can change the course name, and we can also change the short name. However, before you do, it might be worth checking with your Moodle Administrator, in case the students are being automatically enrolled in your course:

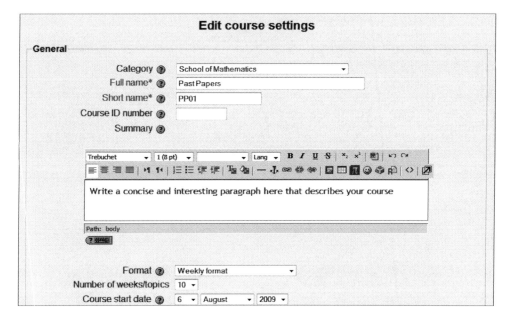

3. Summarize your course in the **Summary** box. The course summary is displayed whenever the course is listed:

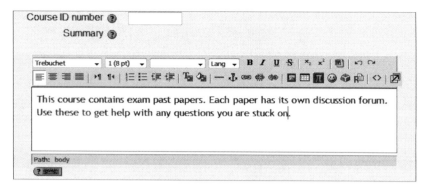

4. If you want to change your course format from displaying weeks to topics, then you need to click on the **Format** drop-down menu:

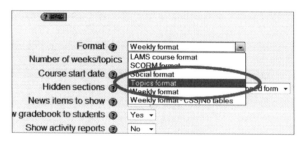

5. To change the number of weeks or topics in your course, click on the **Number of weeks/topics** drop-down menu.

6. When you are happy with the new settings, scroll down to the bottom of the page and press the **Save changes** button. Your course will be reconfigured accordingly:

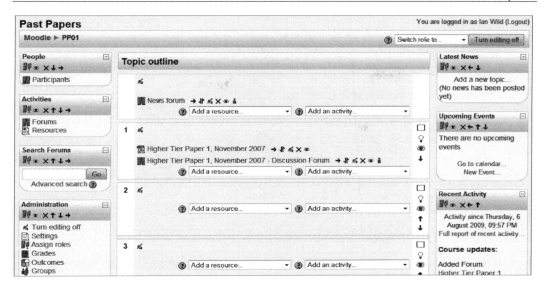

What we have learned so far

To recap, I have uploaded a past paper to my Moodle course and have included an online discussion forum that allows students to discuss problems online between themselves and me.

One of the questions my students seemed to get stuck on involved a ladder pitched against a vertical wall. You are given the ladder's length and the distance between the bottom of the wall and the foot of the ladder. The question asks you for the height of the top of the ladder from the ground. It's a Pythagorean Theorem question, and my idea is to create a Moodle course specifically covering the Pythagorean Theorem. My Moodle admin has created the course and I've been given the **teacher** role. In the rest of this book, we'll be working together to create this course.

Summary

Our journey with Moodle Mathematics has just begun, yet we've already learned a lot about how we can use Moodle to support our mathematics teaching.

Specifically, we've covered the following:

- The advantages of converting mathematics teaching over to Moodle, both from a teacher and student point of view.
- How to upload a past paper to a Moodle course. Keep in mind that I could have uploaded any digital file to my course. I just have to make sure my students have the software to open the file on their computers.
- How to create an online discussion area.
- Basic course configuration settings.

One of the issues we had when my students and I were making forum posts was that we struggled to include even basic mathematics notation. In fact, we hit the very problem with mathematical notation that I described right at the start of this chapter. Let's spend the next chapter solving the problem.

2
Getting Started with Mathematical Notation

In Chapter 1 we began converting our teaching over to Moodle. We uploaded a past paper and complemented that with a forum—an online discussion area. At the end of the previous chapter, I mentioned that my students and I were struggling to include mathematical notation, so in this chapter we will learn how to include mathematical notation in our Moodle courses. There are two ways of including math notation: by using third-party equation editors (for example, the Equation Editor included in Microsoft Office) or by using built-in Moodle "filters". We will be investigating both third-party equation editors and the Moodle Algebra Filter (of all the special math filters included in a basic Moodle installation, the Algebra Filter is the easiest to configure and use).

In this chapter we will learn the following:

- How equation editors can be used to create mathematical notation
- How Moodle writes its own mathematical notation using the Algebra Filter

Let's begin by looking at the third-party equation editors.

Equation editors

A great way to include complex notation in your Moodle course is to use an equation editor. The two readily available editors discussed in detail in this section are as follows:

- Microsoft Equation Editor—ships with all versions of Microsoft Office
- OpenOffice.org Math—if you're not a Microsoft Office user and want to create complex math notation for free, then this is a great choice

Microsoft Office Equation Editor

Microsoft Equation Editor is a program that's bundled free in Microsoft Office. I'm currently using Word 2003. Let's open the Equation Editor and create our first equation.

How to use the Equation Editor

The Microsoft Office Equation Editor is very easy to use. The trick is first finding it:

1. Open Microsoft Word. Create a new **Web page** document:

2. From the main menu, select **Insert | Object**. The **Object** dialog is displayed. Scroll down the list of different object types until you find **Microsoft Equation 3.0**:

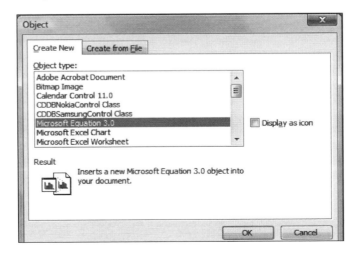

3. Press the **Equation** editor button. The Equation editor and toolbar are displayed (note that your Equation toolbar may be docked):

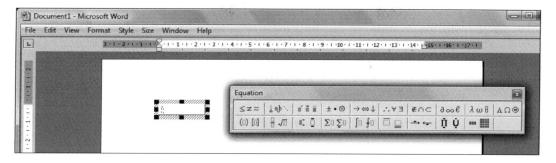

4. Let's edit a fraction. In the **Equation** toolbar, click on the **Fraction and radical templates** button:

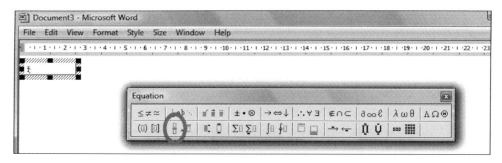

5. Click on the full size vertical fraction button:

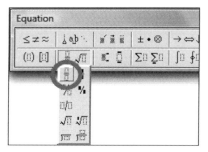

6. Type in the required numbers or letters for the fraction's numerator and denominator:

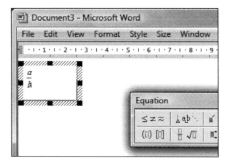

7. Click anywhere in the document to close the Equation editor. We've now created our equation:

8. Let's now save this file. From the main menu select **File | Save As**. In the **Save As** dialog select **Web Page (*.htm; *.html)** as the file type. Remember to give the file a memorable name and to save it somewhere sensible.

 When you press the **Save** button you may get a **Warning** dialog. If you do, then ignore it and press the **Continue** button.

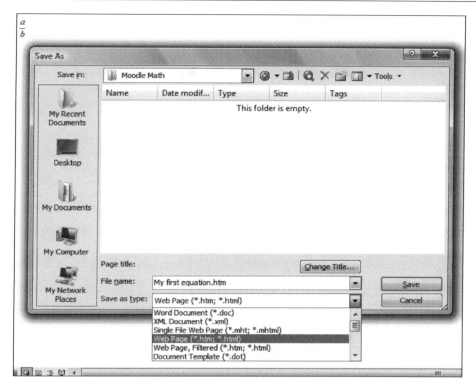

9. Browse to the directory containing the web page you just created. Not only will you see an HTML file, but you'll also see a directory with the same name (suffixed with `_files`):

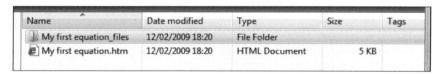

Name	Date modified	Type	Size	Tags
My first equation_files	12/02/2009 18:20	File Folder		
My first equation.htm	12/02/2009 18:20	HTML Document	5 KB	

10. Browse into the `_files` directory. You'll see, among the other files, one or more GIF images. Each image corresponds to an equation you inserted into your original document. Try opening an image now:

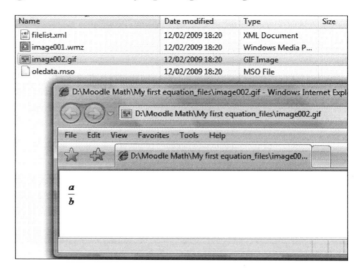

11. That's it: we're done!

 Are you a Microsoft Word 2007 user? Then, to gain access to the Equation Editor you will need to click the **Insert** tab, and then click on the **Object** button. Select **Microsoft Equation 3.0** in the **Object type** list and click **OK**.

You should now be able to start editing your new equation.

Copying equations to Moodle

We need to extract the images from a Microsoft Word document and upload them to Moodle. I'm not really interested in the web page I just created in Word, but rather the images embedded in it. I'm going to copy the GIF files from the web page into another, separate folder. I might even rename the files to help me manage them more easily.

The files duly extracted, we know that the images are saved as GIF files and we can include those images directly in the course. Let's do this now:

1. Navigate to where you want to include your math notation in your Moodle course. I'm currently putting together a Moodle web page (**Add a resource... | Web page**) all about fractions:

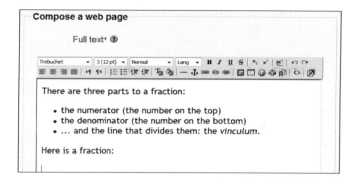

2. Click on the **Insert Image** button in the HTML Editor toolbar:

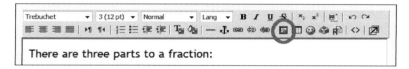

3. In the **Insert Image** dialog, press the **Browse...** button and navigate the **Open** dialog to the location of the GIF files we've just created. Make sure you select the right file. If you're using a Windows computer, then you could select **Tiles** from the **Views** menu to help you select the correct image the first time:

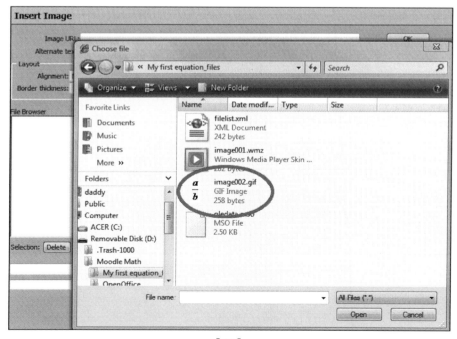

4. Once the notation has been inserted, click on the **Save** button and **display** button, and we're finished!

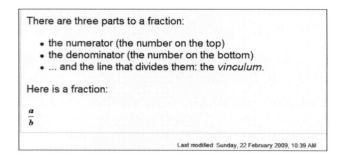

Creating equations with the Microsoft Equation Editor—recap

We've just extracted images containing math notation from a web page, which we created using Microsoft Word, and then we embedded them in our Moodle course. This isn't necessarily the most effective way of including mathematics in your course, but it's certainly the quickest if you are used to using Microsoft Word to create your teaching materials.

Grabbing math notation with the Print Screen (PrtSc) key

Is finding the process of creating a web page and extracting the image proving cumbersome? Is the quality of rendering not up to scratch? One great solution is to simply take a screenshot of the document in Microsoft Word using the Print Screen (*PrtSc*) key and then to use an image editor (for example, MS Paint in Windows) to cut out and save the math as an image. Try this now. On Windows, press the *PrtSc* key (you may have to press the *Shift* key, too), open **Paint** (under **Accessories**) and select **Edit | Paste** (or alternatively, from the keyboard, press *Ctrl + V*). Insert the image in your course following the method outlined above.

Microsoft Equation Editor resources

There are plenty of resources to guide you in the use of Microsoft Equation Editor. Here are just a few:

- Visit the Microsoft Office pages at `http://office.microsoft.com` and search for "equation editor" for plenty of hints, tips, and the best practice from Microsoft itself.

- Design Science, Inc. (http://www.dessci.com)—the home of the makers of Microsoft Equation Editor. They produce the professional version of Equation Editor, called MathType. We'll be encountering MathType in a later chapter.

- For those who need it, Wikipedia (http://en.wikipedia.org/wiki/Equation_Editor) has detailed information on format compatibility and more links to further resources.

OpenOffice.org Math

Are you an OpenOffice user? Then, like Microsoft Office users, you'll also have a formula editor installed—it's called OpenOffice.org Math. Rather than being a drag-and-drop style, WYSIWYG (What You See Is What You Get) editor, the Open Office editor includes a TeX-like linear typesetting editor (if that makes no sense to you, then you'll understand what I mean by this shortly).

Let's run through the process of creating the math notation for a Pythagorean Theorem example (finding the missing length in a right-angled triangle). As you'll see, the process is much the same as for Microsoft Word:

1. Open OpenOffice.org Writer and, if necessary, choose **File | New** from the main menu. Slide across and select **Text Document**.

2. From the main menu, select **Insert | Object | Formula**:

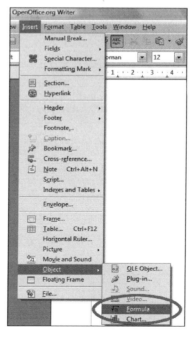

3. The Math equation editor is displayed. The top-half of the window is a drag-and-drop style WYSIWYG editor and the bottom-half a linear text editor, where your equation can be edited using a TeX-like typesetting language:

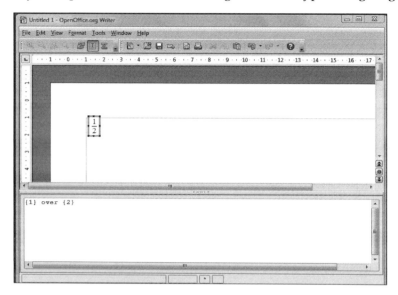

4. To use the drag-and-drop editor, you need to show the **Selection** dialog. To make sure this is turned on, choose **View | Selection** from the main menu. The **Selection** dialog is now displayed:

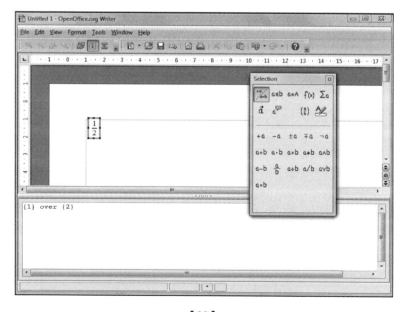

5. Use a combination of the **Selection** dialog and the text editor at the bottom of the screen to construct your equation. For example, to construct:

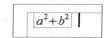

   i.   I click on the addition (+) button in the **Selection** dialog:

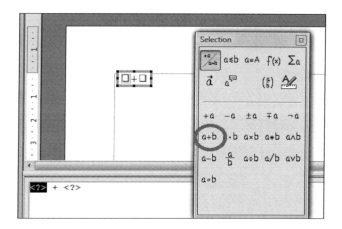

   ii. Using the editor at the bottom of the Math editor window, I then replace:

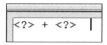

   with the following:

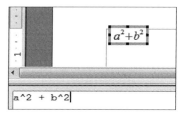

6. After a little further editing my formula now appears in the document as:

$$a^2 + b^2 = c^2$$

7. Next, we need to save the document as a web page. That way, OpenOffice will convert our math notation into images for us. Close the equation editor by clicking anywhere in the document (other than on an equation). Select **File | Save As...** from the main menu.

8. In the **Save As** dialog, ensure you have "HTML Document (OpenOffice.org Writer) (.html)" selected from the **Save as type:** drop-down menu.

9. Choose a suitable name and location for your math notation and click on the **Save** button. Your math notation has now been converted into GIF images:

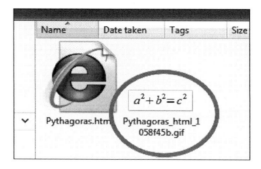

10. Now we're ready to import this math notation into Moodle. Simply follow the instructions in the previous section (*Copying equations to Moodle*).

Creating math notation in OpenOffice—recap

We've used OpenOffice.org Math to create a fragment of math notation that we can then embed into a Moodle course. We saw that the Math editor has a slightly different user interface to Microsoft's Equation Editor. Math incorporates a linear TeX-like editor at the bottom of the window. Using OpenOffice is a great alternative if you don't have access to a copy of Microsoft Office.

Equation editors: Hints and tips

Here are just a few tips when using equation editors:

- You can use different colors for emphasis.

- When including an image of math notation in your course, don't forget to change the alt-text to something sensible, especially if you have a visually impaired student enrolled in your course.

- Create all your equations in one document, and then upload all of the images to Moodle in one handy ZIP file. For more information on this process, check out *Moodle Course Conversion: Beginner's Guide* (ISBN 978-1847195241).

Ideas to try—create an animated equation using Microsoft PowerPoint

Demonstrate solving an equation using an animated PowerPoint presentation. Simply create images of each stage using the processes we've already outlined and add them to your presentation. Try enhancing your presentation with engaging transitions. Certainly, don't forget to use color for emphasis. If this is a presentation that students can look at in their own time, then it might be worth recording an audio commentary. We'll be learning how to create engaging mathematical content using PowerPoint in the next chapter.

Problems with equation editors

The issue with equation editors is that you need to copy the equations from the equation editor to Moodle, rather than creating them *in-situ*. That's the power of Moodle's built-in filters. Let's spend the rest of this chapter investigating basic support for mathematics notation using the Algebra Filter.

Configuring and testing the Algebra Filter

First we need to switch on the Algebra Filter. Because you are going to be reconfiguring your Moodle, you'll need to be logged in as an administrator.

Here's how to switch on the Algebra Filter:

1. From the **Site Administration** block, click on **Modules | Filters | Manage filters**:

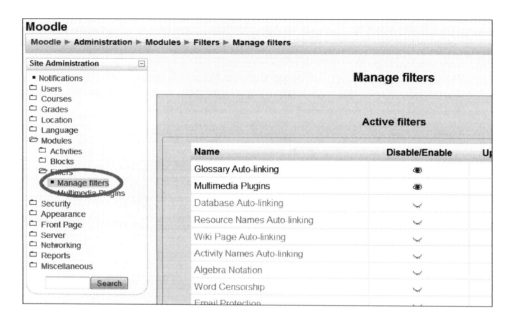

2. Look for the **Algebra Notation** filter. If this filter is disabled, then the eye in the **Disable/Enable** column is shut. Click on the eye to enable the filter:

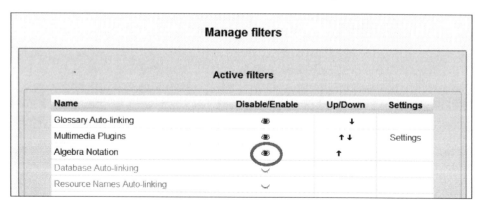

3. Now we need to test that the filter is working correctly. Go to a course front page. Ensure editing is turned on. Click on the **Edit summary** icon:

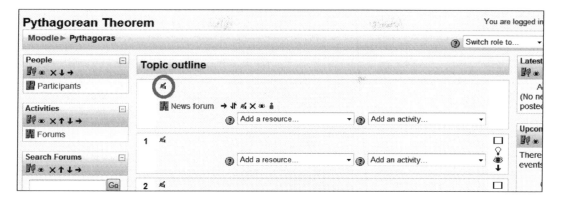

4. Try typing the following text into the HTML editor:

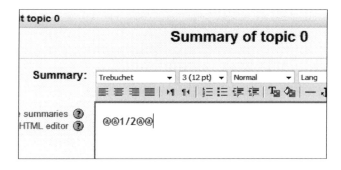

5. To save your changes, click on the **Save changes** button.

6. After we save our changes, if all is well then a simple fraction is displayed as shown:

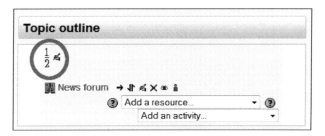

Algebra Filter troubleshooting

What if, instead of a fraction, you see the following error:

Let's check the Algebra Filter's special debug page. To open this page, you will need to visit `http://www.yourmoodlesite.com/filter/algebra/algebradebug.php`. Remember to replace `www.yourmoodlesite.com` with the name of your Moodle. Here is a screenshot of the Algebra Filter debugger page:

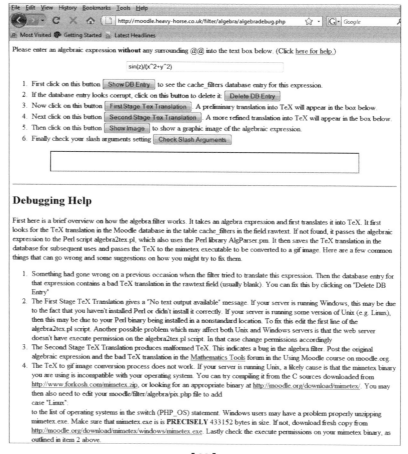

Let's take a quick action to fix the Algebra Filter. Using the debugging screen will certainly help us to track down the error.

Debugging the Algebra Filter

I'm going to follow the instructions on the Algebra Filter debug page in order to determine the problem I'm having with mathematics notation not being displayed:

1. When I press the **Show DB Entry** button, I find the database entry is empty:

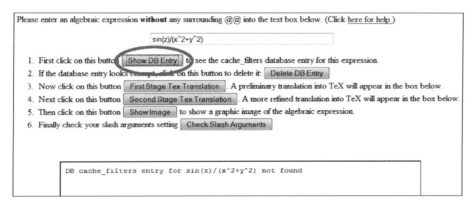

2. The database entry being empty means I can skip step 2 and move straight on to pressing the **First Stage Tex Translation** button:

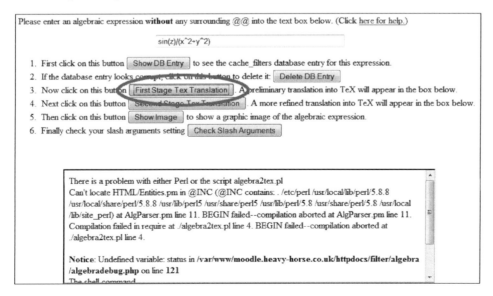

3. You can see from the above screenshot that the Algebra Filter is having a problem converting **sin(z)/(x^2+y^2)** into mathematics notation because it can't locate **HTML/Entities.pm**. I'm going to install this on my server now. You'll see in the following screenshot that we're running an Ubuntu server. You'll need to check the documentation on CPAN.org for more information on the requirements for Windows and Mac servers:

```
The programs included with the Ubuntu system are free software;
the exact distribution terms for each program are described in the
individual files in /usr/share/doc/*/copyright.

Ubuntu comes with ABSOLUTELY NO WARRANTY, to the extent permitted by
applicable law.

To access official Ubuntu documentation, please visit:
http://help.ubuntu.com/
Last login: Thu Jan 22 22:37:31 2009 from 79-67-34-105.dynamic.dsl.as9105.com
ian@heavyhorse:~$ sudo apt-get install libhtml-parser-perl
Be careful!
[sudo] password for ian:
Reading package lists... Done
Building dependency tree
Reading state information... Done
The following extra packages will be installed:
  libhtml-tagset-perl liburi-perl
Suggested packages:
  libwww-perl
The following NEW packages will be installed:
  libhtml-parser-perl libhtml-tagset-perl liburi-perl
0 upgraded, 3 newly installed, 0 to remove and 0 not upgraded.
Need to get 0B/208kB of archives.
After this operation, 782kB of additional disk space will be used.
Do you want to continue [Y/n]? y
Selecting previously deselected package libhtml-tagset-perl.
(Reading database ...
```

4. We also need to check that the Algebra Filter files have the correct permissions. This tends to be a problem on Unix servers (where the permissions should be 755):

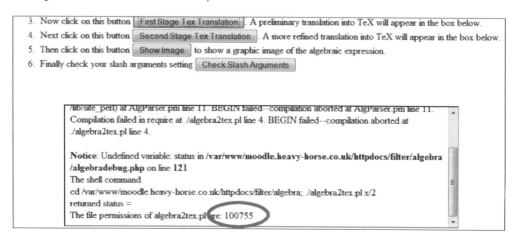

5. Now click your browser's refresh button. The Algebra Filter debug page is reset, and you should now be able to work your way through each step of the debug process. When you eventually click on the **Show Image** button, is the math notation displayed correctly?

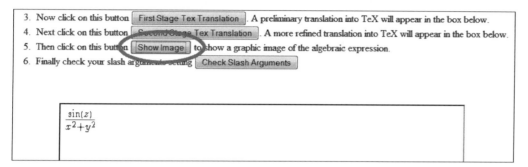

Debugging the Algebra Filter—recap

We have been using the Algebra Filter debug page to determine why mathematics notation is not being displayed correctly. We ensured that file permissions were correctly set, which is a common problem. We eventually found that the source of the problem was that some of the support files the Algebra Filter needs to function were not correctly installed on the server. This is also another common problem.

Algebra Filter—details on implementation

The Algebra Filter is a "sub filter", as it were, of the TeX filter. It requires the file filter/tex/lib.php to render TeX as images. There's more on the TeX filter in later chapters. That the Algebra Filter uses the TeX filter may mean that we need to set correct permissions for the executable files that the TeX filter uses—that's mimetex.exe on Windows environment, mimetex.linux for Linux, mimetex.darwin for Darwin, or mimetex.freebsd for FreeBSD.

Troubleshooting on shared hosting

If your Moodle is on shared hosting (that is, your Moodle instance is one of many instances running off the same computer somewhere on the Internet) then the chances are you won't have the ability to do as I did and simply install new components on the server. If this applies to you and you are still having problems getting the Algebra Filter to work, then you will need to contact your Moodle host. Don't worry if you do get stuck trying to get the Algebra Filter to work. We'll investigate some good alternatives to the Algebra Filter, which can also work on shared hosting, later on in this book.

If all else fails...

In this case, we will either join the Mathematics Tools forum on Moodle.org (`http://moodle.org/mod/forum/view.php?id=752`), which is where you'll find me and the rest of the Moodle community who specialize in Moodle's support for mathematics notation, or in the Text Filters forum (`http://moodle.org/mod/forum/view.php?id=1510`), which is where you'll find discussions on Moodle filters in general.

How the Algebra Filter works

In order for Moodle to support math notation, we need to enable special filters that spot mathematics included in the text that we type into the HTML editor (that's what filters do, they filter your text for anything interesting). The filter we are using (assuming our admins have turned it on) is called the Algebra Filter. You'll have probably noticed that this filter detects mathematics surrounded by @@ characters. The concept of laying out math notation via special text-based codes is called "typesetting".

Typesetting mathematics

The notation you are including within the @@ characters is a kind of typesetting system called ASCII Math. The Algebra Filter then converts this into yet another kind of system called TeX (pronounced 'tek'). The filter then generates an image in GIF format, and for the sake of accessibility (at least for those users who know TeX), the alternative text of this image is the TeX version of the mathematics notation you originally typed in. Hover the mouse pointer over the image or right-click on the image and check its properties:

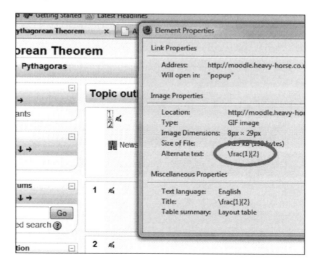

The fraction $\frac{1}{2}$ written in TeX is indeed \frac{1}{2}. If this doesn't make much sense then don't worry; there's much more about TeX in later chapters, and I'll be showing you how you can create math notation without having any special typesetting skills at all.

Algebra Filter examples

In the following table you'll find just a few examples of math notation typeset using the Algebra Filter and the resulting output produced by Moodle:

Expression	Generated output
`@@1/2+1/3 = 3/6+2/6 = 5/6@@`	$\frac{1}{2}+\frac{1}{3}=\frac{3}{6}+\frac{2}{6}=\frac{5}{6}$
`@@sin(pi/2)=1@@`	$\sin\left(\frac{\pi}{2}\right)=1$
`@@x^2-4=(x+2)(x-2)@@`	$x^2-4=(x+2)(x-2)$

For more information on the Algebra Filter, check out the Algebra Filter page in the online Moodle documentation at `http://docs.moodle.org/en/algebra_filter`.

Experimenting with the Algebra Filter

I've started to develop my Pythagorean Theorem course. I've included the mathematical representation of the theorem in the **Topic outline**. See if you can re-create it:

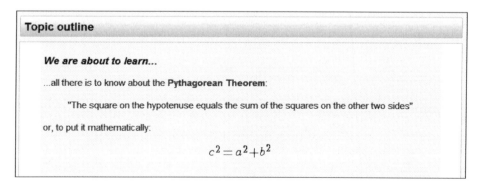

Summary

In this chapter we saw how we could use our Microsoft Word or OpenOffice.org Writer skills to create math notation using their respective, built-in math equation editors. Although using a word processor to generate the notation was fairly straightforward, the process of creating math notation in one application and uploading it into another can become involved. That's why we investigated Moodle's built-in Algebra Filter to generate math notation in-situ.

Specifically, we covered these topics:

- Creating math notation using Microsoft Equation Editor
- Using OpenOffice.org Math to create math notation
- How to switch on and use Moodle's built-in algebra notation filter, including plenty of examples of how to configure and use that filter to get you started

This chapter concentrated mainly on administrative tasks: we don't want to forget that converting our math teaching over to Moodle means we can create math courses that are entertaining and engaging. In the next chapter, we'll look at how to create a mathematical PowerPoint presentation and convert this to Moodle.

3
Enhancing Your Math Teaching

In this chapter, we will be looking at taking our current resources and converting them over to Moodle. There have been plenty of books written on how to take your current resources and convert them over to Moodle (I've written one: *Moodle Course Conversion: Beginner's Guide*, ISBN 13 978-1-847195-24-1 by Packt Publishing). Because this book is dedicated to math teaching, I'm going to concentrate on the kinds of resources we math teachers usually have. They usually come in two flavors. The first are the "static" resources: PowerPoint presentations, documents provided by publishers (such as resources provided on a CD-ROM at the back of a textbook or downloadable from the publisher's website). In this chapter, we'll focus on these static resources. Again, those are the resources math teachers and lecturers usually like to convert to Moodle. The other type of resources are "interactive" resources. We'll be investigating these in later chapters.

In this chapter we will learn the following:

- How to create math-related PowerPoint presentations and, using the content sharing website SlideShare, include them in our Moodle courses along with a suitable narration
- How to extract math-related videos from YouTube and include them in our courses
- What a screencast is and how it can be used to explain mathematical concepts

There are many topics to explore in this chapter, so let's make a start with mathematical PowerPoint presentations.

PowerPoint and Mathematics

We have already seen how we can use the Microsoft Equation Editor to include mathematics notation in Microsoft Word documents (we copied them from the document into our Moodle course). Microsoft PowerPoint also includes the Equation Editor, and we can use this facility to create some quite elegant online explanations of difficult mathematical ideas. Here is a quick recap (using Microsoft PowerPoint instead of Microsoft Word):

1. Click the slide to which you want to add an equation.

2. On the **Insert** menu, click **Object**.

3. In the **Object type** list, click **Microsoft Equation 3.0**
    (if Microsoft Equation 3.0 is not listed, then you will need to install it.
    See http://support.microsoft.com/kb/228569).

4. In the Equation Editor, use the buttons and menus to type your equation.

5. To return to Microsoft PowerPoint, on the **File** menu in Equation Editor, click **Exit**.

The equation will now be included on your slide.

Add a special Equation Editor button to any Microsoft Office application toolbar. For example in Office 2003, in the **View** menu, point to **Toolbars**, and then click **Customize**. Click the **Commands** tab, and in the **Categories** list, click **Insert**. In the **Commands** box, click **Equation Editor**, and then drag it from the **Commands** box to a gray area within any toolbar. Then click **Close**. Click on the new toolbar button to install and display the **Equation Editor**.

Quickly crafting a Pythagorean PowerPoint

I'm guessing you're going to be fairly familiar with PowerPoint, so let's make a start by creating a basic presentation, showing our students how they can transpose/rearrange an equation. I'm going to be showing my students how they can find the missing length in a right-angled triangle. Note that I'm an Office 2003 user running Windows Vista. If you aren't using the same version of Office or the same operating system as me, then as you follow my examples your screen might look different from mine:

1. The first step is to create a new presentation. For the first page of this presentation, I've added a new slide and used the Title, Text, and Content layout:

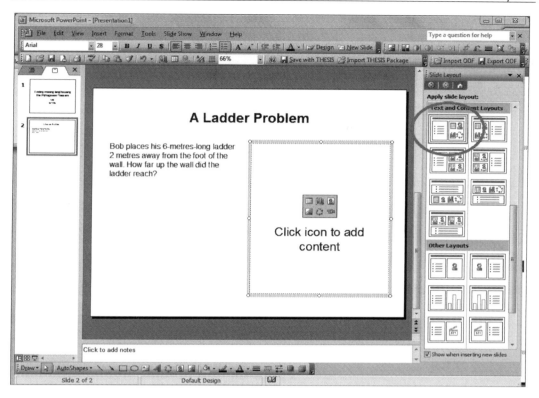

2. I've searched for a Creative Commons image of a ladder on Flickr and drawn a schematic using Microsoft PowerPoint's built-in drawing tools. Here is the completed slide:

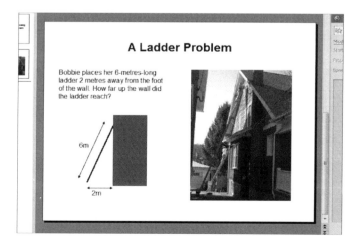

3. In the next slides, let's demonstrate how we can turn the ladder problem into a Pythagorean Theorem/algebra problem (without being too scary about the algebra). Let's animate the slide to allow the students to recall the theorem:

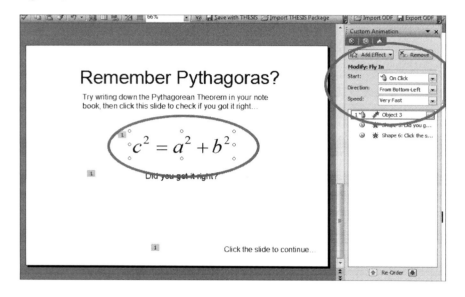

4. Now, allow the students to check if they got it right. Right-click on an object and select **Custom Animation...** to make the presentation a little more interactive:

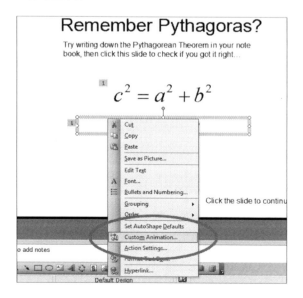

5. Now I've recalled the Pythagorean Theorem, which I need to relate back to the ladder problem. Again, I've used animations to make the slide interactive:

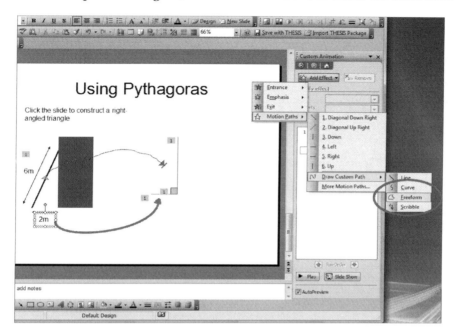

6. I'm going to complete the presentation by giving my students a little guidance on algebraic transposition and then that's it—I'm done!

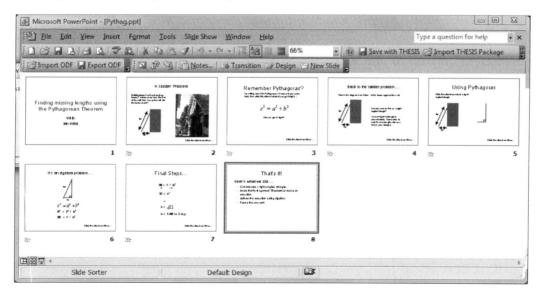

I hope you'll agree that with some simple custom animations we've made this PowerPoint far more engaging and entertaining than it would otherwise be.

Want to avoid creating a truly boring PowerPoint presentation? Navigate your browser to http://www.youtube.com and search for Don McMillan's video on how NOT to use PowerPoint!

But what's the best way to include the presentation in my Moodle course? That's the subject of the next few sections.

Uploading to Moodle

I could simply upload the PowerPoint as is to my course files area, but I'm a bit worried that without my describing what's going on in the presentation, it isn't going to make a lot of sense to my students. To overcome this problem, I'm going to record an audio commentary.

You can insert sound directly into your slides either from the main menu (**Insert**) or via the **Insert** tab in Microsoft PowerPoint 2007's ribbon.

Providing an audio commentary

The presentation I crafted in the previous section is fine on its own, and I do use something similar as part of my face-to-face teaching. But I want my students to be able to study this example in their own time and, to that end, I would like to enhance it with an audio commentary. There are three basic ways I can achieve this (aside from inserting audio into each slide). Each has its own advantages and disadvantages:

- Record a separate audio track and allow the students to listen to the audio following the presentation at their own pace—almost like a read-along story

- Upload the presentation to SlideShare and use SlideShare's built-in audio recording tools to narrate the PowerPoint

- Record a screencast. Either upload it directly to our Moodle course or to a content sharing website (that is, YouTube or TeacherTube)

In the following sections we'll investigate each option in turn.

Recording a separate narration—using Audacity to narrate a slideshow

A great way to record a narration is by using **Audacity**. Audacity is an extremely popular, free recording and audio editing tool. Download the latest version from `http://audacity.sourceforge.net/download/`.

Once you have Audacity installed, it is very easy to use. Let's record a narration:

1. The first task, before we begin recording, is to write a script. There's nothing worse than listening to a badly prepared or rambling presentation, so let's make sure it's tightly scripted:

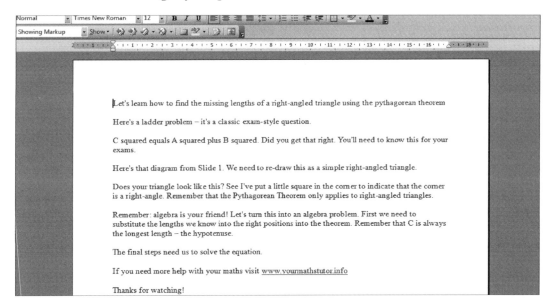

2. When you are ready to begin recording your commentary, press Audacity's "record" button:

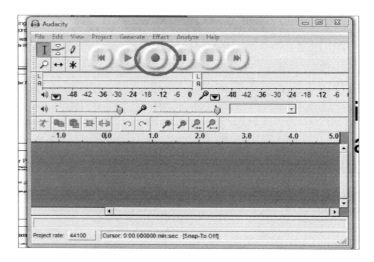

3. When you are finished recording, press the "stop" button. Don't worry about making mistakes or there being pregnant pauses because we can easily edit these out in the next step. When you have finished, the recording is displayed:

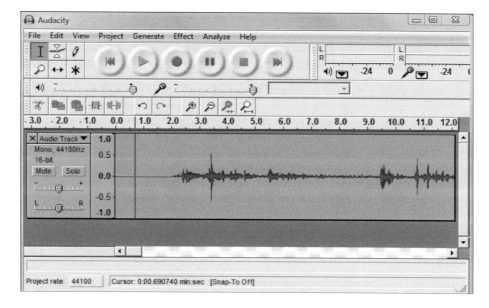

4. Audacity is loaded with many great audio editing features, so by way of an example, I'm going to pick just one: **Fade Out**. Use the selection tool to select the final segment of your recording:

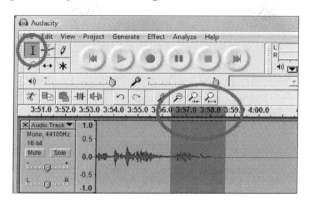

5. From the main menu, select **Effect | Fade Out**. Try experimenting with some of the other audio options that are available:

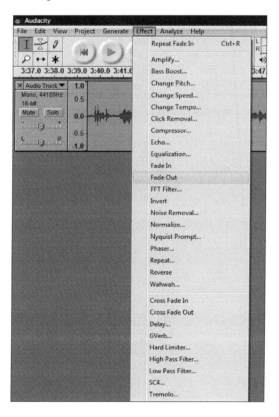

6.   When you are happy with your recording, you'll need to save it. From the main menu, select **File | Export as MP3...**.

7.   Choose a suitable filename and location and click on the **Save** button.

8.   Complete the ID3 Tag dialog:

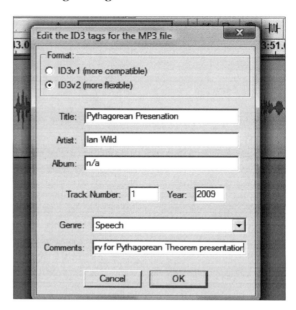

9.   Hit the **OK** button and Audacity creates your new MP3 file. That's it. We're done!

Recording a narration—recap

When my PowerPoint is included in my Moodle course, it will be viewed by students who won't have the benefit (or curse) of my commentary when I am giving my face-to-face teaching. It would be great if we could also include an audio commentary so that students can follow the presentation in their own time, at their own pace. To that end we've just used the free audio recording and editing tool, Audacity, to create an audio commentary for our PowerPoint presentation.

Audacity can't export an MP3 file: Lame_enc.dll not installed

Did you see the following warning when you attempted to save your recording as an MP3 file?

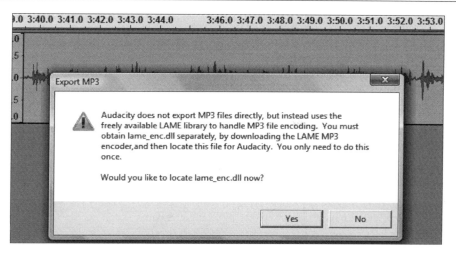

If so, then you need to install LAME. Here's how:

1. For the LAME download page you will need to visit `http://audacity.sourceforge.net/help/faq?s=install&item=lame-mp3`.

2. I'm using Audacity on Windows, so I need to download the file `Lame_v3.98.2_for_Audacity_on_Windows.exe`.

3. Once downloaded, you can run the **LAME for Audacity Setup Wizard** as shown:

4. Once LAME is installed, you need to let Audacity know where it is. Recall the Export MP3 warning dialog? To the question **Would you like to locate lame_enc.dll now?** answer **Yes**.

5. Use the **Where is lame_enc.dll?** dialog to locate the LAME file:

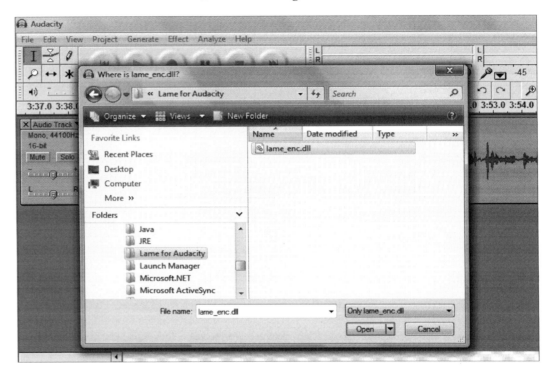

You'll now be able to create MP3 files as described in the Recording a separate narration—using Audacity to narrate a slideshow section.

Adding sound effects to your recording

Sound effects can make a presentation far more engaging and entertaining. For example, when talking about triangulation to locate an enemy gun position (a geometry exercise), I've complemented the presentation with the sounds of battle. Microsoft PowerPoint 2007 comes with its own sound effects library. These are part of the sound clip organizer.

Providing a "Next Slide" cue

Did you ever listen to read-along stories when you were young? When it was time to turn the page there was a beep or a sound effect added into the commentary. Audacity makes it easy for us to do the same (ideal for younger children). Follow these steps to include a turn-the-page beep:

1. Ensure the cursor is positioned at the correct time in your recording.

2. From the main menu, select **Generate | Tone...**.

3. Configure your tone settings. Here is a typical example (a short burst):

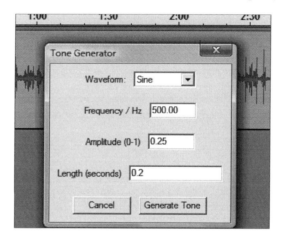

4. Click on the **Generate Tone** button. Your audio cue is inserted.

Including your presentation and audio file in a course

As this book isn't really aimed at the novice Moodle user, the basics of including resources in Moodle courses is something you should be fairly familiar with. (If not, refer to Chapter 1 of this book or, for a more comprehensive investigation, *Moodle Course Conversion: Beginner's Guide*, ISBN 13 978-1-847195-24-1 from Packt Publishing.) How am I going to include the presentation and audio commentary in my Pythagorean Theorem course? There's a topic in my Moodle course dedicated to exam practice. In that I've added a Moodle web page:

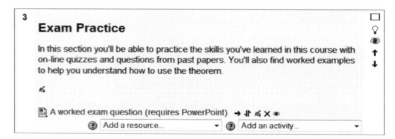

And in that I've provided links to both the presentation and the audio file:

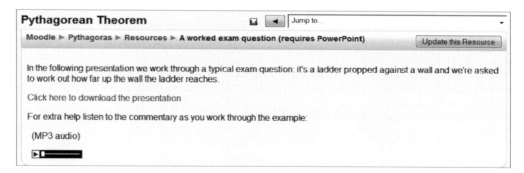

 The embedded audio player is automatically inserted by Moodle if the Multimedia filter is enabled for MP3 files. You might need to ask your Moodle admin to turn this on for you.

Here's how to create the Moodle web page shown in the previous screenshot:

1. I've composed the web page text, and I'm ready to include links to the presentation and the audio:

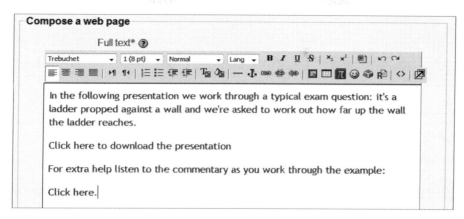

2. I've selected the text **Click here to download the presentation** and then clicked the **Insert Web Link** button. The **Insert Link** dialog is displayed:

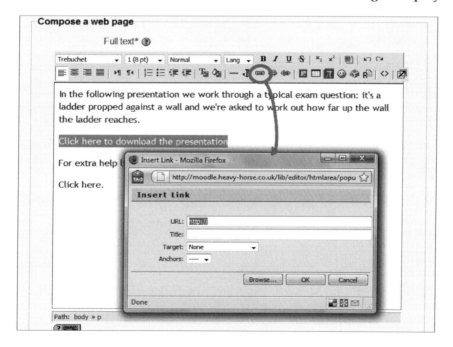

3. On clicking the **Browse** button, a new dialog opens displaying the course files area. From there you can upload both your presentation and audio files:

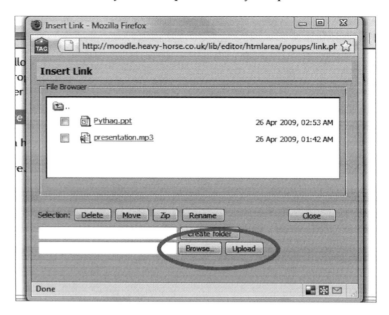

4. I'm going to click on **Pythag.ppt** to select it. The **Insert Link** dialog is updated accordingly. I want the presentation to open in a new window (so that clever browsers don't try to open up the presentation in the browser window and make it look as though my Moodle has disappeared). I've also specified a link title for those students of mine who are visually impaired:

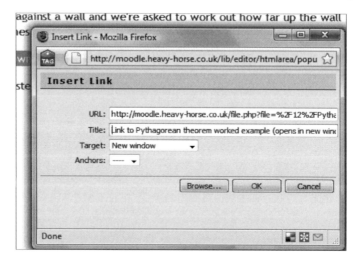

5. Click on the **OK** button. The text has now been converted into a link. You can't click on the link as of now:

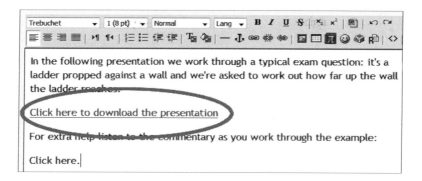

6. Repeat this for the audio file. Scroll down to the bottom of the page and click on the **Save and display** button. The link now works, and assuming the Multimedia filter is configured correctly, an audio player has been embedded:

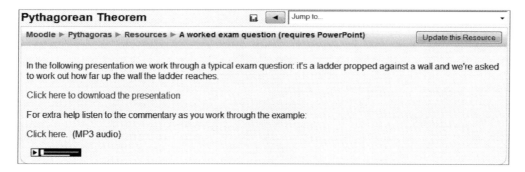

7. To remove the **Click here** link above the audio player, we need to modify the web page HTML code slightly. To start, click on the **Update this Resource** button at the top of the page.

8. In the **Compose a web page** box, click on the **Toggle HTML Source** button in the HTML editor. The web page code for the Moodle web page will be displayed:

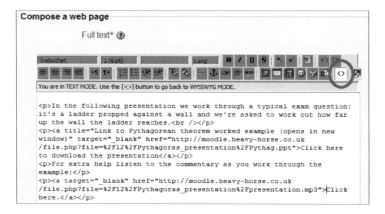

9. Locate the text **Click here**:

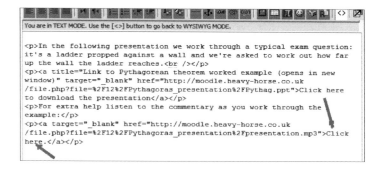

10. When you've found it, simply delete it. Scroll down to the bottom of the page and click on the **Save and display** button. The "Click here" link above the audio player has now been removed, but the player is still displayed:

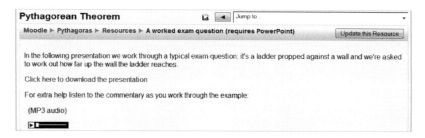

11. That's it. We're done!

Creating a Moodle web page for your presentation and audio narration—recap

When it comes to playing audio, enabling the Multimedia filter will ensure Moodle includes its own audio player on the page. This will overcome potential problems with students not having suitable audio playback software installed on their computers or, more commonly, their playback software not being set up correctly.

There are problems with simply uploading a PowerPoint presentation as is. The first is that your students may not have PowerPoint installed on their computers. The second is that presentations can be quite large and, therefore, difficult to share. Have you heard of content sharing websites like YouTube (for sharing videos) or Flickr (for photographs)? Similarly, there's a site dedicated to sharing presentations called SlideShare. If you're worried about plagiarism when you start sharing your presentations, then there's no need to be concerned; you can choose who to share your presentations with.

Uploading to SlideShare

Navigate your browser to `http://slideshare.net`. You'll need a SlideShare account. Once you've logged in you'll be able to upload your presentation:

1. Select **My Slidespace** from the menu at the top of the page:

2. Click on the **Upload your first slideshow now** link:

3. Use the **Upload** page to choose your presentation and upload it to SlideShare:

4. Once the file is uploaded, you can specify how it can be shared. Note that you can choose to make the presentation private (you don't have to make it available to the entire world):

5. When you are done with the details, click on the **Publish** button. The presentation needs to be converted so that SlideShare can display it correctly. This can take a while, but you can check the status to see how SlideShare is getting on:

6. Once the presentation has been converted, it's ready to view:

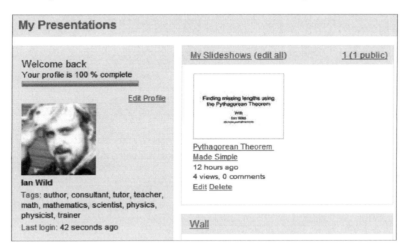

7. That's it! The presentation is online and ready to go.

Here are just a few of the advantages of using SlideShare to include your presentation in a Moodle course:

*   Your students may not have PowerPoint installed on their computers nor be aware of the special player they can download (check out the Microsoft website for details). That's no problem! SlideShare will play the presentation for them.

*   You don't have to worry about file sizes. The presentation is stored on SlideShare's computers and not in your Moodle.

*   Using SlideShare's built-in tools, it's easy to create an audio commentary (more on this in the next section).

But there can be disadvantages. For example, I tried making my presentation more engaging and entertaining by including animations (which is good if you are a visual/spatial learner). However, in SlideShare those animations no longer work.

So, how do you actually include a SlideShare presentation in a Moodle course? Let's do this now:

1. SlideShare provides a fragment of web page code along with each presentation:

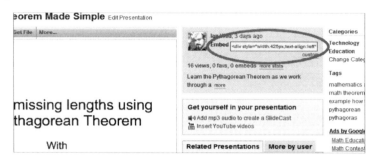

2. Right-click on the code, and choose **Select All** followed by **Copy**.

3. In your Moodle course, you can include the slideshow using the HTML editor. I'm going to include the presentation on a Moodle web page. Click on the **Toggle HTML Source** button:

4. Cursor to the end of the page's HTML code, right-click and select **Paste**:

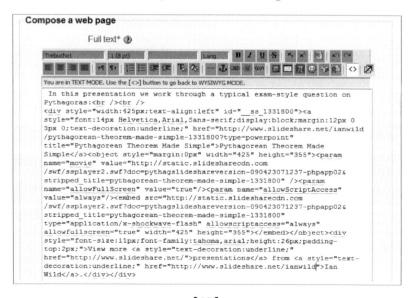

5. Click on the **Toggle HTML Source** button again and the slideshow gets displayed in the editor:

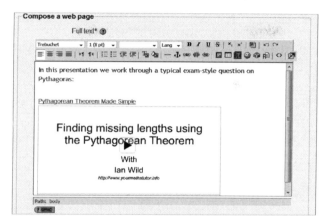

6. It's that simple!

Look for embedded code in your favorite content sharing websites (for example, YouTube). Including YouTube videos will be discussed later in this chapter.

Audio commentaries and SlideShare—slidecasts

We've already seen how we can record an audio commentary using Audacity. I've mentioned that you can create an audio commentary (or slidecast) using SlideShare. Let's do that now. I can use the recording I made previously to narrate the presentation uploaded to SlideShare:

1. Return to your my slidespace area. Click on the **Edit** link under your presentation:

2. On the **Edit Slideshow Details** page, click on the **Create Slidecast** tab:

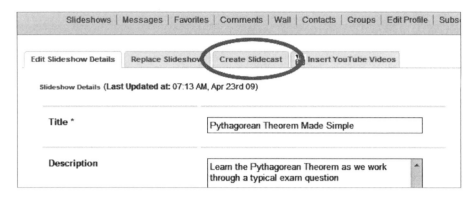

3. The **Create Slidecast** page is displayed. As the instructions on this page recommend, you will need to upload your commentary to the Internet. You won't be able to use Moodle, as your course files area isn't accessible outside of Moodle (that's one of Moodle's vital security features). I'm going to upload my narration to the Internet Archives You'll need a registered account to do this. Simply follow the instructions to upload your file:

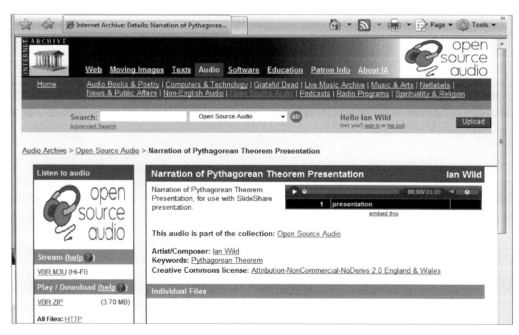

4. Copy the link to the audio file to the Create Slidecast page (if you are using the Internet Archive, then the individual audio files are listed at the bottom of the archive page). Click on the **Link mp3 to slideshow** button:

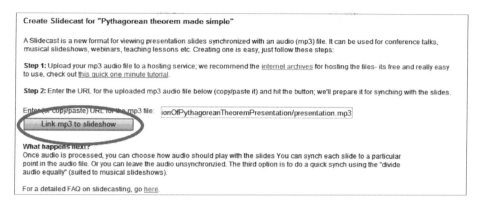

5. Once the audio is processed, the **Synchronization Tool** is displayed. Use the tool to associate a slide with the correct fragment of audio:

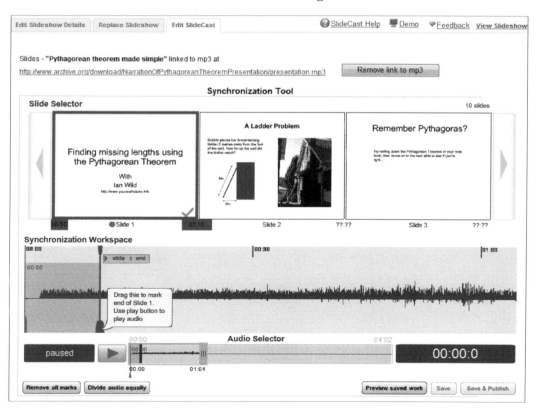

6. Once you are happy with your new slidecast, click on the **Save & Publish** button in the bottom-right corner of the page:

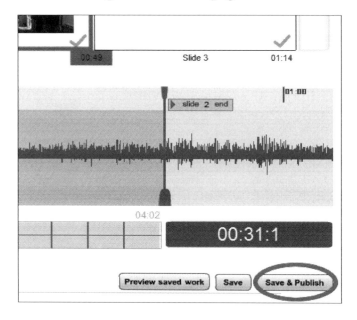

7. Return to your My Slidespace page. Click on your presentation. You will now see a note in the corner of the presentation:

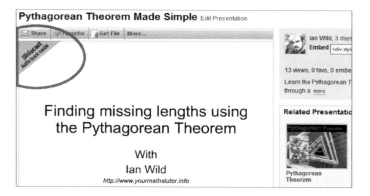

8. That's it. We're done!

Before we leave our discussion of SlideShare, make a note of the SlideShare sidebar. If you've more than one presentation in your course, it can make finding the right presentation easier for your students. Visit `http://www.slideshare.net/widgets/blogbadge` for more details.

Converting PowerPoint to Moodle—more options

So far, we've just been uploading our PowerPoint presentations as is (as a PPT file). That's not the only way. Here are a few more options:

- **Convert to a PDF**: You will need Microsoft Word 2007 or later, OpenOffice or a PDF printer installed. Remember that you may lose those pretty animations and transitions, so it is best to try the conversion first to test the result.

- **Convert to images**: This is a good option if you don't want students to cut and paste text.

- **Convert to web pages**: You can also cut and paste text into Moodle web pages.

- **Convert to Flash video**: A free conversion tool called **iSpring** is available from **iSpringSolutions** (`http://www.ispringsolutions.com/products/ispring_free.html`). The great thing about iSpring is that it preserves your animations.

- **Convert to SCORM**: It isn't free, but a popular tool for converting presentations to SCORM is THESIS (`http://www.getthesis.com`). We'll be investigating SCORM in the next chapter.

Preparing your presentation for Moodle is described in detail in *Moodle Course Conversion: Beginner's Guide*, ISBN 13 978-1-847195-24-1, and *Moodle 1.9 for Teaching 7-14 Year Olds: Beginner's Guide*, ISBN 13 978-1-847197-14-6, both available from Packt Publishing.

Including YouTube videos

Do you want to include a video in your course? There is a plethora of video sharing websites available (see `http://en.wikipedia.org/wiki/List_of_video_sharing_websites`), but the most popular has to be YouTube. There are dozens of Pythagoras-related videos on YouTube, and one that always keeps my classes entertained is *Darth Vader Explains the Pythagorean Theorem* by Mister Teacher (also known as John Pearson) from `learnmegood.com`:

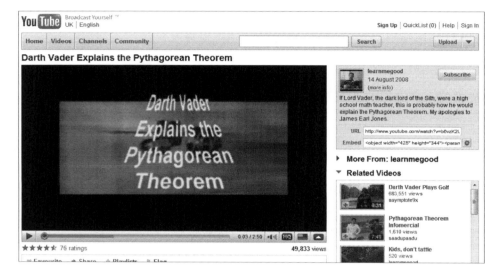

The problem I have is that, although I can get access to YouTube at school, my students can't (my staff login is different from a student account). How do we overcome that problem? The best way is to extract the video from YouTube and upload it to our course files area. We can then link to it and have Moodle embed a video player, just as it did with its own audio player in the previous section. Here's how to achieve this using `Keepvid.com`:

 Your Moodle admin will need to enable the FLV filter in the multimedia plugin to have Moodle embed the video player in your Moodle page.

1. I've got the *Darth Vader Explains the Pythagorean Theorem* video open in my browser. I'm going to open a browser window (you could use another tab if your browser supports them) and navigate that window to `http://KeepVid.com`:

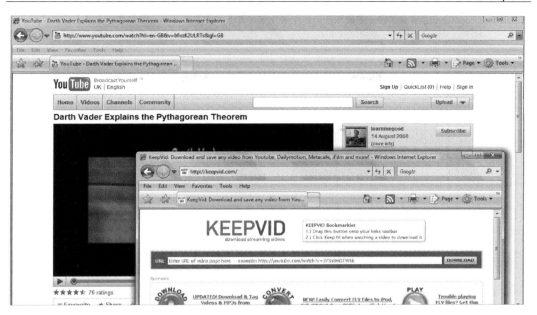

2. Copy the web address of the page in YouTube containing your video into KeepVid's **URL** edit box:

3. Click on KeepVid's **DOWNLOAD** button. You will be provided with a set of links allowing you to download the video to your computer:

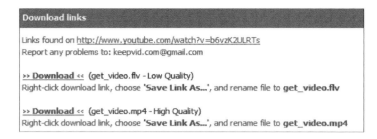

4. I'm going to download the **Low Quality** FLV file and rename it accordingly. Once downloaded to your computer and renamed, upload it to your course files area. I'm uploading the file via a web link on a Moodle web page:

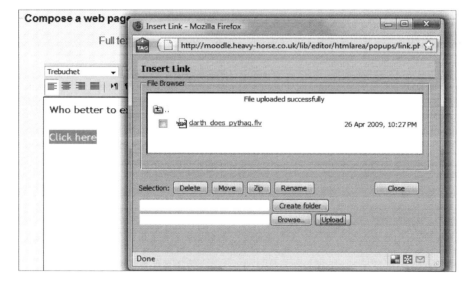

5. For more details on how to create the link, see the "Including your presentation and audio file in a course". Once the link is created, Moodle can recognize it as a link to a video and embed a video player:

6. It's as simple as that! If you would rather have the video without the associated **Click here** link, see Linking to a PowerPoint presentation and Audio file.

YouTube videos—recap

With my staff account I can access YouTube videos that my students, with their restricted logins, can't access using the college computers. So, I've used the free, online service `KeepVid.com` to extract a great video explaining the Pythagorean Theorem from YouTube and included it in my course. Before doing so, I've checked with the video's creator to make sure that's ok with him (and Mister Teacher has kindly let me use his video in this book). Because my Moodle admin has enabled the FLV filter in the Multimedia Plugins module, Moodle has spotted the link to the video and automatically included a video player in the page.

Looking for a video sharing website dedicated to educational content? Check out TeacherTube at `http://teachertube.com`.

Don't get caught out with copyright

As a matter of courtesy if nothing else, you should always ask the permission of the creator of the video before including it in a course. For example, I emailed Mister Teacher to ask if it was possible to include his video in this book. If you are not sure about copyright and licensing, then consult the librarian or information officer employed by your establishment if one is available.

Creating screencasts

Never finding exactly the right video to include in our courses might lead us to wondering how we can create our very own math videos. One option is to do what many teachers and lecturers seem to do: set up a camera in front of your interactive white board and record yourself giving a short lesson on a math topic. If, like me, you are a little camera-shy and don't really want to be onscreen (and not wanting to give your students the opportunity of having fun with your face in Photoshop), then a good alternative is to record a screencast—a recording of your desktop as you describe what you're doing on it. That could be, again, narrating a PowerPoint presentation or, more usefully, if you have a graphics tablet you could be narrating working through a math problem as you draw it onscreen. If this is an option you would like to explore, then Jing (a free, cut-down version of the popular Camtasia Studio software) is available for Windows and Macs (`http://jingproject.com`). If you are a Linux user, then recordMyDesktop (`http://recordmydesktop.sourceforge.net/about.php`) and Xvidcap (`http://xvidcap.sourceforge.net/`) are popular options. If you're thinking about video editing software and you are a Windows user, then look no further than Windows Movie Maker—the free movie editing software that comes as standard. If you're a Mac user, you'll have access to i-movie. For general ideas and guidance on Windows Movie Maker, check out *Moodle 1.9 for Teaching 7-14 Year Olds*, ISBN 13 978-1-847197-14-6.

Incorporating third-party content

Publishers are becoming more aware of virtual learning environments (VLEs), like Moodle, and they are beginning to provide materials in VLE-friendly formats. For example, most documents are provided in PDF format (publishers like this format because files can be copy protected), activities are provided in SCORM or Flash format (more on SCORM and Flash in the next chapter). The formats publishers choose are nearly always generic, and it would be unusual if your students needed to install special software on their computers in order to view it. If you aren't sure of the format of files you want to upload, then it's well worth checking with your admin.

Avoid uploading large documents to your Moodle course. Your Moodle's file upload limit might prevent you from doing this. (In versions of Moodle prior to 2.0, you are not warned if you are going to exceed the limit before the upload commences.) Furthermore, your students won't be happy if they have a slow Internet connection and it's a large file you are expecting them to download.

Summary

In this chapter, we focused on converting static resources over to Moodle—of the kind we math teachers typically want to move online. Specifically we covered the following:

- Creating math-related PowerPoint presentations and, using the content sharing web site SlideShare, including them in our Moodle courses along with a suitable narration
- Extracting math-related videos from YouTube and learning how to include them in our courses
- What a screencast is and how it can be used to explain mathematical concepts

After looking at static resources, let's think about the interactive resources we can convert to Moodle, specifically Flash and SCORM activities. This will be the subject of the next chapter.

4
SCORM and Flash

This chapter sees us continuing to enhance our courses, although this time with more advanced multimedia resources and activities. This chapter is going to concentrate on two specific types of technology: SCORM and Flash. Why? Because these are the formats that are easiest to include in course management systems. That means if you are a content provider, then supplying your resources as SCORM or Flash means that they can be used in any course management system (you don't have to worry about producing content dedicated to a specific system). Either format has its own advantages and disadvantages, which we will learn as we advance through this chapter.

In this chapter we shall look into the following:

- Learn what SCORM is and how we can include SCORM resources in our courses
- Explore Flash technology and how Flash can enhance our courses

Although what I have said so far makes it sound like this chapter is going to be technology led, the emphasis is on what the different technologies can provide and how each brings a different type of enhancement to our Moodle course. The technology that was specifically developed to support the packaging together of online learning resources and activities was SCORM, so let's start with learning what SCORM is and what it can do for us.

SCORM

You may well have come across SCORM resources and not realized it. Commercial content producers are providing online resources and activities as SCORM objects. For example, the very popular—and free—Fling the Teacher from ContentGenerator. net allows you to export the Fling the Teacher game in SCORM format. The idea is that the SCORM content will work regardless of which VLE you happen to be using. So, what is SCORM?

SCORM actually stands for **Shareable Content Object Reference Model**, and it's a technical standard telling authors how their content should be structured so that VLEs can display it without any hassle. The great thing is that the standard also describes how a student's progress through the activities and quiz results can be published to the VLE. This means that Moodle can remember how far a student has progressed, and the results of any tests built into a SCORM object can be included in the course grade book.

What to learn more about SCORM and Moodle?

Check out the forum on Moodle.org dedicated to SCORM (http://moodle.org/mod/forum/view.php?id=1951). There is a simple introduction to SCORM here: http://moodle.org/mod/forum/discuss.php?d=3757#p18828

Where to find free SCORM content

Using your favorite search engine to seek out "free SCORM course" in your subject area will probably draw a blank, and you'll find many commentators on the Internet complaining about this. The problem is that you need to know exactly what to look for. In fact, we don't want to search for SCORM. What we are actually looking for is the Open eLearning Content Repositories. A great place to start your search is at WikiEducator.org (http://www.wikieducator.org/Exemplary_Collection_of_Open_eLearning_Content_Repositories). For example, if you are in the UK and teach students who are aged over 16 then your college might have signed up to the **National Learning Network (NLN)**: http://www.nln.ac.uk/Materials/default.asp. The NLN provides a wealth of free educational content.

Remember to check out the license agreement before you include SCORM content in your course.

The Moodle.org site also contains a database of free SCORM objects, which we can download and experiment with in the SCORM Repository (http://moodle.org/mod/data/view.php?id=7198). To learn a little more about SCORM and what it can do, I'm going to download a sample SCORM object from the repository (not specifically related to Pythagoras for the moment). I'm going to experiment with the SUMS Maths Fraction Monkeys game (http://moodle.org/mod/data/view.php?d=50&rid=2056), provided free courtesy of SUMS ONLINE (www.sums.co.uk).

Adding SCORM to a course

Let's start by learning how to add the Fractions Monkeys SCORM object to our course. Our first step involves downloading the game from `Moodle.org` and then uploading it to our course files area:

1. Download the Fractions Monkeys game directly from `http://moodle.org/ mod/data/view.php?d=50&rid=2056`. The link to the SCORM object is in the bottom right-hand corner of the page:

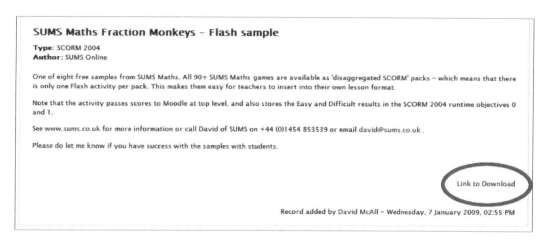

2. Return to your Moodle course and, from the course **Administration** block, click on **Files** to open your course files area:

3. Create a new folder named **SCORM** in your course files area, and upload the game to this folder:

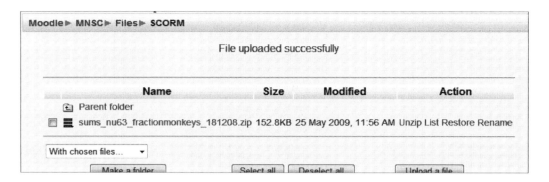

4. Return to your course's front page. Make sure you have editing turned on, choose a topic, and click on the **Add an activity...** drop-down menu. Select **SCORM/AICC** from the list:

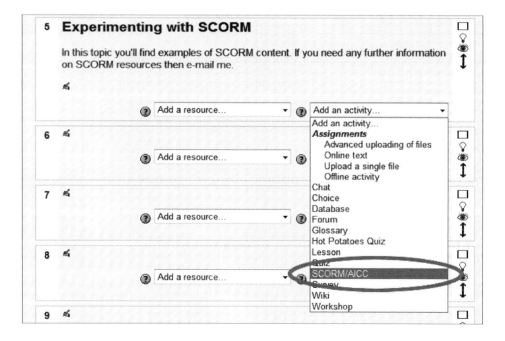

5. Give the new activity a name and complete the summary (Moodle will complain if you don't). Next, we need to select the SCORM package we just uploaded to the course files area. Click on the **Choose or upload a file...** button:

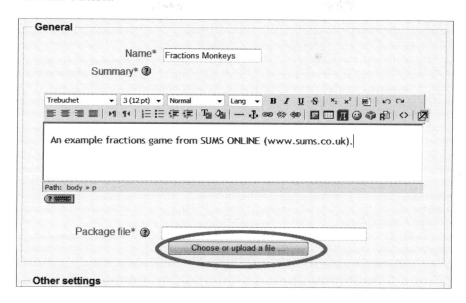

6. Navigate to the SCORM package you just uploaded and, under **Action**, click on **Choose**:

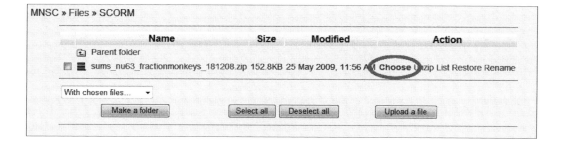

7. Scroll to the bottom of the page and click on the **Save and display** button. The contents of the Fractions Monkeys package will now be displayed. To test that the SCORM package has been included correctly, click on the **Enter** button at the bottom of the page:

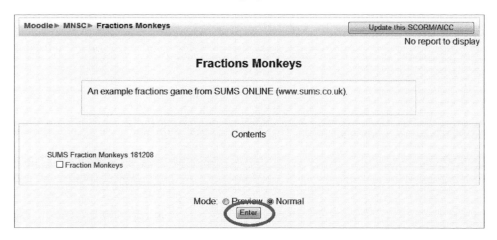

8. Now we can play the game:

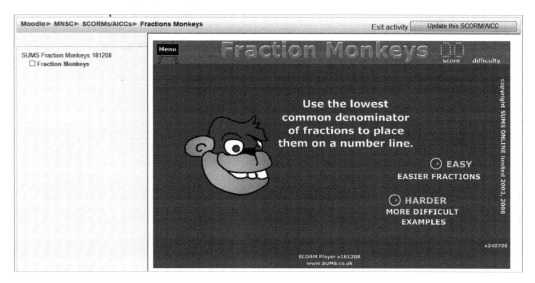

Now we've included our first SCORM activity in our math course. We've seen that it's a two step process: first we need to upload the SCORM package to the course files area, and then we need to add a SCORM/AICC activity to the course and choose the file we've uploaded.

Display options

One of the most common problems you will encounter when you first start experimenting with SCORM objects is that they often don't quite fit in their window (the bottom and/or right-hand side of the activity is cut off):

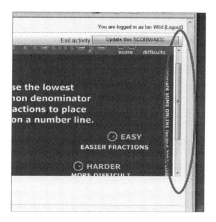

Don't worry! We have full control over how the object is displayed. The area in which the object is displayed is called the **stage**. Here's what happens if your stage size is too small:

1. Click on the **Update SCORM/AICC** button.

2. Scroll down to the **Other settings** box and under **Stage size**, specify the **Width** and **Height** of the stage:

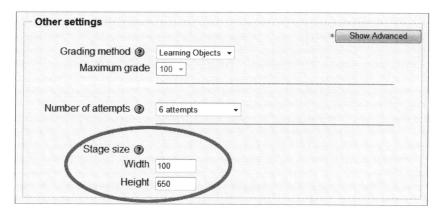

You might need to experiment with these settings until you are happy.

SCORM and the grade book

What's great about SCORM activities (and its one advantage they have over Flash) is that the results get included in the course grade book. Return to your course front page and click on **Grades** in the course **Administration** block. You'll see your SCORM activity listed. As students attempt the activities contained in the package, the grades are recorded automatically:

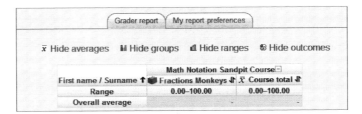

SCORM packages can contain more than one quiz. If that's the case, how is the overall grade calculated? We can configure how the overall grade is calculated by returning to the SCORM activity settings page. Scroll down to the **Other settings** box and choose the **Grading method** from the drop-down menu:

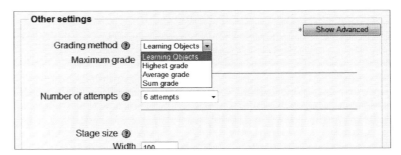

The table below describes our grading options:

Grading method	Description
Highest grade	The course grade book will record the highest grade achieved by students as they work through all the activities in the SCORM resource.
Average grade	The arithmetic mean of the scores from the activities contained in the SCORM package is recorded in the course grade book.
Sum grade	All the scores from all the activities contained in the SCORM package are added together and recorded in the grade book.
Learning Objects	The activities contained within the SCORM resource are called 'learning objects'. The number of completed/passed objects will be recorded in the course grade book.

DIY SCORM

If you don't want to rely on third-party SCORM learning objects, or maybe you want to create your own learning objects to share with other colleagues (maybe they aren't using Moodle as their VLE), then you will want to be creating your own SCORM packages. There are two ways to achieve this. One is to use free or open source tools. The other is to use commercial products. We'll spend the rest of this section looking at the most popular of both options.

Creating SCORM for free

The two most popular free SCORM package creation tools are eXe and Udutu. eXe is an editor that you download. Udutu is an online tool. Let's start by investigating eXe!

eXe (eLearning XHTML editor)

The eXe (eLearning XHTML editor) is a free tool available to download from the eXeLearning website (`http://exelearning.org`). To download the eXe tool, you will need to click on the relevant link on the eXeLearning website main page. Once downloaded, simply run the installer and follow the instructions. When you first run the eXe application, you are presented with an empty project:

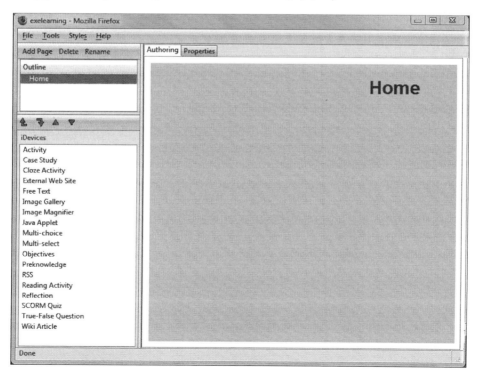

Let's create a new SCORM package all about the Pythagorean Theorem. We'll start by configuring the eXe project:

1. Click on the **Properties** tab in the authoring window, immediately under the main menu:

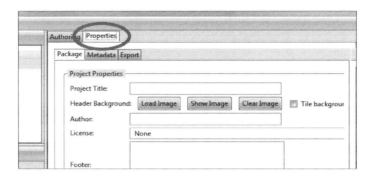

2. Complete the project details by giving the project a title and specifying who the author is. You can also specify a background image. I've found a picture of the island of Samos, where Pythagoras came from, in the Wikipedia entry for Samos:

3. When you have configured all the settings, remember to scroll down to the bottom of the page and click on the **Apply** button. If you wish, that same information can be included in the project's metadata (click on the **Metadata** tab). I would recommend doing this if you are going to be making your project available for general distribution. When you are finished, click on the **Authoring** tab.

4. In the **Outline** pane, double-click on **Home**. We can now rename that to something more relevant:

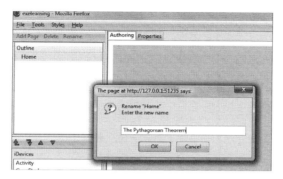

5. The **iDevices** pane lists the activities we can include in our SCORM package. I'm going to add some text onto the first page. From the **iDevices** pane, select **Free Text**:

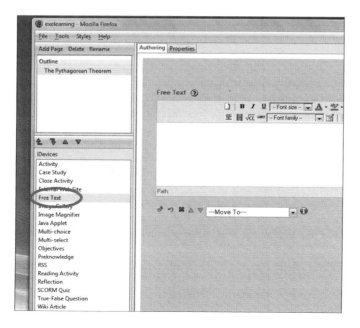

6. Use eXe's HTML editor to edit the text. Just like Moodle's own HTML editor, the eXe editor allows you to include images and even embed multimedia. What's great for us math teachers is that eXe also contains a built-in math notation editor:

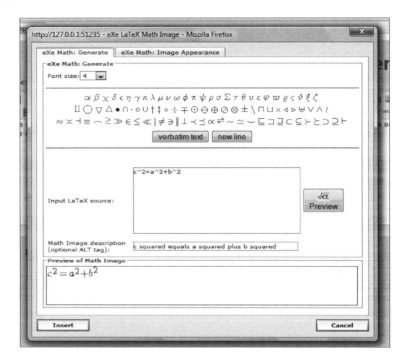

7. When you are happy with your changes, you can commit them by clicking on the tick icon:

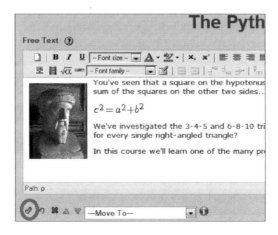

8. To add a new page to your SCORM package, click on the **Add Page** option in the **Outline** pane:

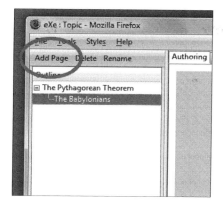

9. See that a page can contain more than one iDevice. In my new page, I've included a **Preknowledge** and a Multi-select iDevice:

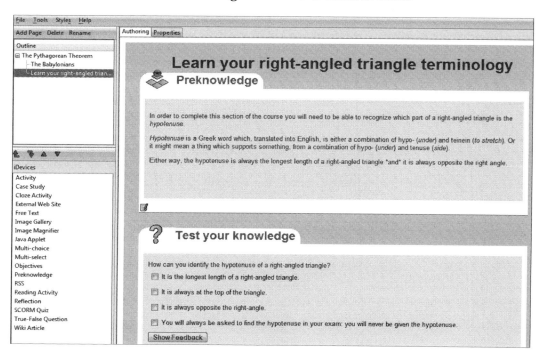

10. To export your finished SCORM package, select **File | Export | SCORM 1.2**:

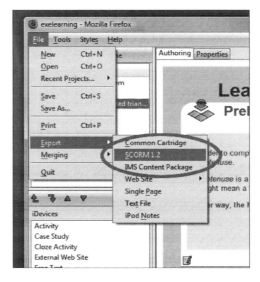

11. Choose a name for your new package. Test your new package in Moodle by following the instructions given earlier in the Adding SCORM to a course section.

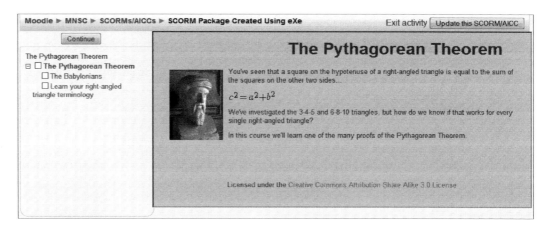

Using eXe—recap

We've just seen how easy it is to create SCORM packages using the free eXe editor. SCORM packages are created by adding pages into your eXe project and adding iDevices onto those pages. You can have more than one iDevice on a page and arrange them as per your requirement. What's great about the resources you create is that they can be included in courses on other VLEs (ideal if you are sharing with colleagues).

Udutu

Udutu is an online SCORM package editor available at `http://www.myudutu.com`. You will need to register to use the myUdutu tool. Constructing courses with Udutu is very much in the same vein as eXe. You create learning objects and arrange them in a course. The fundamental difference is that the creation of content is online. That means you can easily collaborate with colleagues in creating SCORM compliant materials. Once you have created your course, you can export it and upload it to your Moodle course in the usual way.

Create an account at myUdutu and log on. The main page gives you the option to create a new course. Give your new course a name, and click on the **create new course** button:

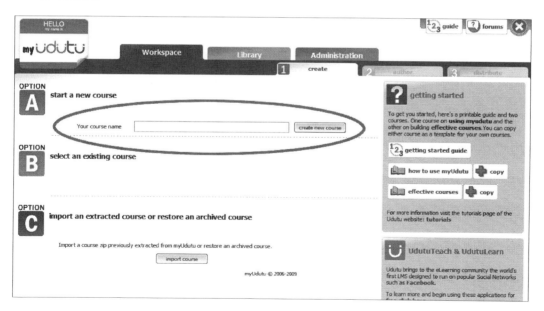

On the next page you are given options to edit the course details. Complete these as appropriate:

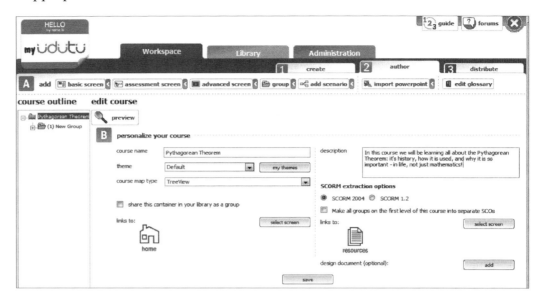

Now you can start adding resources and activities to your course. The types of pages you can add to your course are given across the top of the page:

- **basic** and **advanced**—pages of information (rather like Moodle's web page resource).

- **assessment**—a quiz page. There are many different quiz types to choose from.

- **import powerpoint**—useful if you already have resources created using PowerPoint.

- **scenario**—an action maze, like a Moodle lesson activity.

- **glossary**—same idea as Moodle's glossary activity.

Try out the different types of screens; they are very easy to use. Notice that you can also add a narration to each screen:

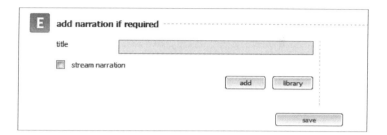

You can choose screens to add from the Udutu library. Click on the green icons next to each screen type to search the library:

To distribute your finished course, click on the **distribute** tab:

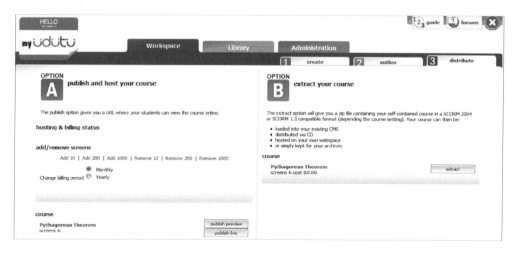

You can either host your course on Udutu or extract your course in SCORM format and upload it to Moodle.

Commercial products

The advantage of commercial products (at the time of writing, at least) is that they provide a very quick way of converting your current teaching materials over to SCORM. For example, if you want a quick way to convert Microsoft Office documents (including PowerPoint presentations) to SCORM for easy inclusion in your Moodle course, then **THESIS** is a good choice (note that Udutu also lets you import PowerPoint presentations). For more details, check out http://www.getthesis.com. Installing THESIS adds two special buttons to your office application toolbars: a **Save with THESIS** button and an **Import THESIS Package** button. Converting your document, spreadsheet, or PowerPoint presentation is as easy as clicking on the **Save with THESIS** button:

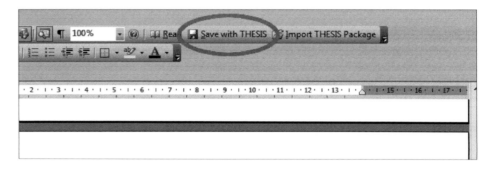

Here are some other popular commercial products:

- Lectora (http://www.trivantis.com)
- ToolBook (http://www.sumtotalsystems.com/products/content-creation/tb_index.html)
- Captivate (www.adobe.com/products/captivate)

You may have been provided with, or bought, a SCORM course related to the syllabus you are teaching.

 SCORM resources can be very big. If you have difficulties uploading the content to your course files area, then check that the package isn't bigger than the maximum file upload size.

A SCORM course

Rather than having a SCORM package included as an activity in your Moodle course, you might want to convert your Moodle course into a SCORM course. Here's how:

1. Return to your course's front page, and click on **Settings** in the course **Administration** block:

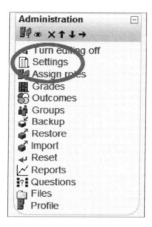

2. Click on the **Format** drop-down menu and select **SCORM format**:

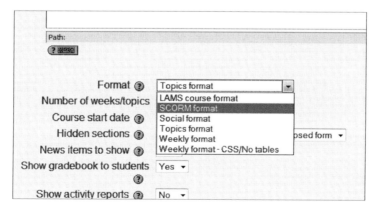

3. Scroll to the bottom of the page and click on the **Save changes** button. Moodle will automatically navigate to the SCORM activity settings page. Choose your SCORM package and configure the activity in the usual way.

4. When a student enrolls on the course, he/she will be taken straight to the SCORM activity.

Configuring a Moodle course to be a *wrapper* for a SCORM course is ideal if you have been provided with (or have bought) SCORM resources that cover certain aspects of your syllabus, which are themselves self-contained courses.

In the next section, we'll briefly look at a fun and engaging alternative to SCORM—Flash.

Being Flash

If you've a game or an online interactive resource that you want to include in your course, then the chances are it's written in Flash. There are plenty of sources of free Flash games and resources out there on the Internet. Here are just a few:

Website	Details
Subtangent.com	Plenty of math games and activities (also includes worksheets and stationery—for example, isometric paper—to print out).
NRICH (http://nrich.maths.org)	Contains problems, articles, and games for learners aged 5 to 19 years.
Woodlands Junior (http://www.woodlands-junior.kent.sch.uk/Games)	Popular web site in the UK packed full of math-related games and activities.
Mathsduck.co.uk	Home of the Duck of Maths. Resources dedicated to the UK's key stages 3 and 4.

A quick search from your favorite search engine will no doubt yield many more.

Including Flash resources in your course

A simple way of including Flash resources in your course is to link to the website containing the game. For example, there is a great Pythagoras game at http://www.kidsnumbers.com/pythagorean-theorem-game.php. I could simply add a resource and choose **Link to a file or website**. If you don't want your students to be wandering off onto the Internet from your Moodle course, then you will need to upload the relevant Flash files to your course files area. Not all websites allow you to download the Flash resources (copyright restrictions may prevent you from having them). Flash files usually have the extension .swf (Shockwave Flash). For example, http://sandfields.co.uk/games provides resources to create Flash games. For example, you can download the Flash files for the Bish Bash Bosh game and upload them to your Moodle course. Details of the process can be found in *Moodle 1.9 for Teaching 7-14 Year Olds* (ISBN 978-1-847197-14-6), also available from Packt Publishing.

Creating your own Flash resources

It is possible to convert your current teaching materials over to Flash. For example, in the previous chapter, we saw how math-related PowerPoint presentations could be uploaded to SlideShare to overcome the problem that not all of our students might have PowerPoint installed on their computers. Another neat way of overcoming this problem is to convert our presentations to Flash movies. One tool for doing this is **iSpring Free** (http://www.ispringsolutions.com). The conversion tool is free to download and easy to use. The advantage of this tool is that all of those fancy transitions and animations you included in your presentation are preserved when they are converted into a Flash resource.

Flash requirements

You and your students will need the latest version of the Flash player installed on your computers (get.adobe.com/flashplayer). It's very unlikely that any of you will not have the latest version installed.

One other point to note is that by default Flash quiz scores are not recorded in the course grade book. For more information on how this can be achieved (and it's not for the faint hearted), check out http://docs.moodle.org/en/Flash_module.

For more information on Flash and Moodle in general, especially concerning Flash best practice, check out Moodle.org: http://moodle.org/mod/forum/discuss.php?d=68233.

Java—a SCORM and Flash alternative

We'll be investigating a very powerful tool written in Java when we install DragMath in Chapter 7. There are many games and activities also written in Java. You'll need the correct version of the Java Runtime Environment (JRE) installed in order for the *applets*, as they are called, to work.

Moodle Ideas: Getting students to create games for your Moodle courses

As a final thought for this chapter, there are plenty of games you can include in your Moodle course. Have you ever considered setting your students the exercise of creating their own online games? For example, both Sandfields Comprehensive (`http://www.sandfields.co.uk`) and ContentGenerator.net (`http://contentgenerator.net`) provide the facilities to allow you to create your own games. It is fun for your students (regardless of age), creative, and they may even get to learn some math along the way!

Summary

In this chapter, we investigated two popular eLearning technologies: SCORM and Flash. Materials produced by commercial publishers are provided in SCORM or Flash format because they want to be sure that they will work in all VLEs. We also learned how we can create our own SCORM and Flash activities. Specifically, we covered the following topics:

- How to include SCORM materials in our Moodle courses and how SCORM activities are recorded in the course grade book.

- How to create our own SCORM activities using both free and commercial tools. These tools can provide an efficient way of converting our current teaching materials over to Moodle.

- What Flash is and how to incorporate Flash games and activities into our courses.

After exploring how to present information to our students and beginning to look at quizzes and tests in SCORM packages, let's move on to learning how we can use Moodle to set math-specific quizzes, which is the subject of the next chapter.

5
Geometry

In the previous chapter, we saw just how easy it was to incorporate SCORM and Flash activities in our Moodle courses. In this chapter we will be including tasks and activities that will allow my students to explore mathematical concepts in a much more hands-on way. Geometry is one topic in mathematics that could benefit from an interactive, online visualization tool that fully integrates with Moodle courses.

Luckily, there is a powerful, free tool we can use to create interactive geometry tasks for our students. It's called GeoGebra, and this is the application we'll be concentrating on in this chapter. What's great about GeoGebra is that there's also a Moodle filter available that allows us to include GeoGebra activities directly into our Moodle courses.

In this chapter we will learn how to do the following:

- Install and use GeoGebra
- Create static GeoGebra worksheets and include these in our Moodle courses
- Investigate dynamic worksheets and learn how these can allow our students to explore geometry interactively
- Create an interactive proof of the Pythagorean Theorem

 Using GeoGebra in your Moodle courses will provide a wonderful opportunity for your students to explore complex mathematical concepts. GeoGebra is a very powerful tool, and this chapter is intended only as a simple introduction. In order to fully appreciate GeoGebra, it is worthwhile making time available to experiment with its many features.

Let's start with a brief introduction to GeoGebra!

About GeoGebra

GeoGebra (http://www.geogebra.org) is a multi-award winning software developed by Markus Hohenwarter. With GeoGebra we can create both static and interactive geometry, algebra, and calculus resources for our Moodle courses. The following is a screenshot of GeoGebra in action (we'll show you how to create this example later in this chapter):

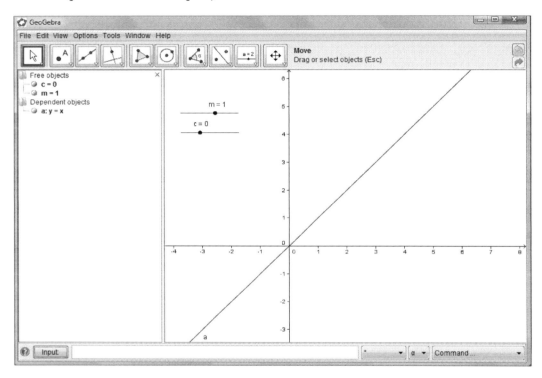

Think of GeoGebra as having two views: an algebra view (on the left) and a graphics view (on the right). What's specified in the algebra view is reflected in the graphics view and vice versa. In this chapter, we will be concentrating on geometry (as my Moodle course is all about the Pythagorean Theorem).

Installing and testing GeoGebra

Without further ado, let's make a start and get GeoGebra installed on our computers. The following instructions provide details on how to install GeoGebra on a Windows computer. At the time of writing, there is no installation for a Mac (you get a ZIP download, and the final application is inside the ZIP).

GeoGebra is a Java application, and it will need the Java Runtime Environment version 1.4.2 or later installed. Also note that if you are attempting to install GeoGebra on your school or college computer, then it might fail if your login doesn't have the correct permissions.

Start by navigating your browser to the GeoGebra home page at `http://www.geogebra.org`:

1. From the left-hand main menu, click on **Download** to open the download page. You can either download a copy of GeoGebra or install a **WebStart** icon on your desktop. Select the **Download GeoGebra** link:

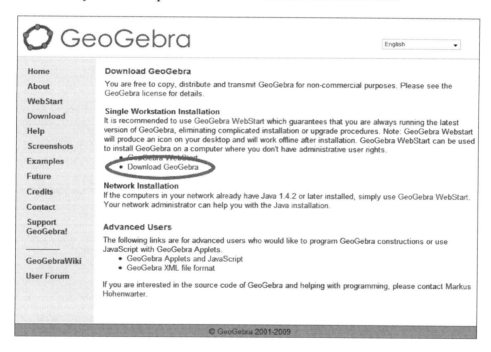

2. You are taken to the GeoGebra download page. The download page attempts to determine which operating system you are using (Windows, Mac, Linux) and recommends the appropriate version of the GeoGebra installer:

3. Click on the **Download** button to download the recommended installer (assuming the download page has managed to determine your OS correctly).

4. When it has finished downloading, run the installer. Note that the installation wizard also requires Java Runtime Environment (version 1.4.2 or later). Choose a **Typical** installation. If you are interested in the components that come as part of the GeoGebra bundle, then click on the **Custom** button and then on **Next**:

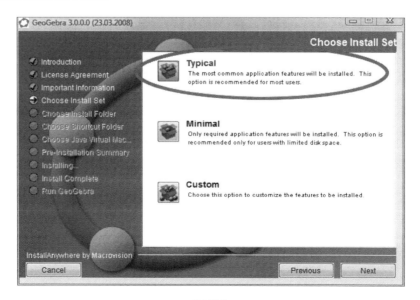

5. When the installation is complete, run GeoGebra. A new worksheet is displayed:

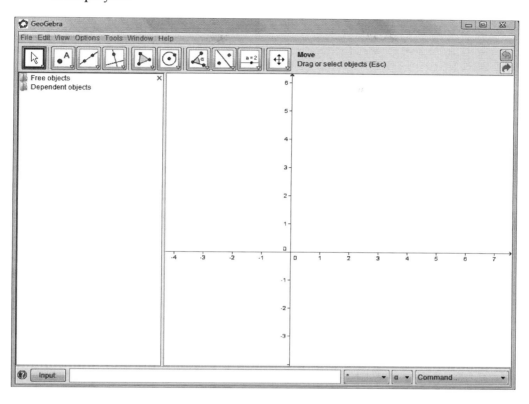

6. On the left is the algebra view, and on the right is the graphics view. We will now insert a function of variables x and y using the text input box at the bottom of the page:

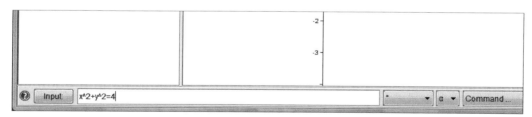

7. The graph of that function is then displayed in the graphics view and listed as a new object in the Algebra view:

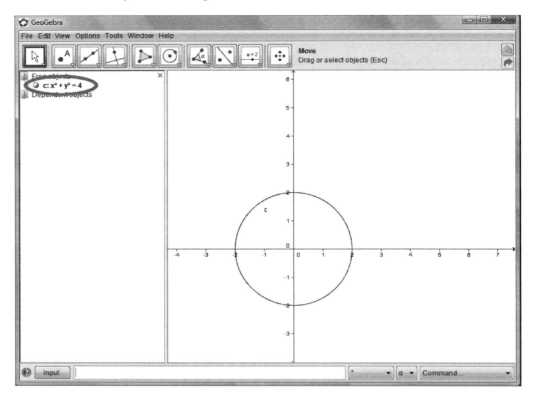

8. You can now save this as a GeoGebra file. Select **File | Save as...** from the main menu. GeoGebra files have the extension .ggb.

Once we've created a GeoGebra file, how do we get that work included in our Moodle course? Fortunately, there's a special plugin we can install, which is the subject of the next section.

Incorporating GeoGebra activities in Moodle

To include GeoGebra files in Moodle, you will need to install the GeoGebra filter. Note that this is a filter looking for links to GeoGebra files, which will replace the links with a GeoGebra worksheet.

Installing the GeoGebra filter—Moodle admins only

Let's install the filter, but remember that you will need to be a Moodle administrator to do so:

1. To download the GeoGebra filter, you will need to visit
   `http://moodle.org/mod/data/view.php?d=13&rid=585&filter=1`.
   This page tells you all about the filter. Look for the **Download latest version** link.

2. The next step is to upload the complete folder "geogebra" into Moodle's
   `filter` folder on your Moodle server. Make sure you set the folder and file
   permissions correctly.

3. Now go back to Moodle, make sure you are logged in with admin privileges,
   and then from the **Site Administration** block choose **Modules | Filters |
   Manage filters**. Enable the **Geogebra** filter:

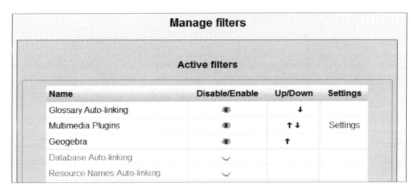

4. Now, let's incorporate the GeoGebra worksheet I created in the earlier
   section. Go to a Moodle course, make sure you have editing turned on, click
   on **Add a resource...**, and select **Compose a web page** from the list. Type a
   short fragment of text into the HTML editor:

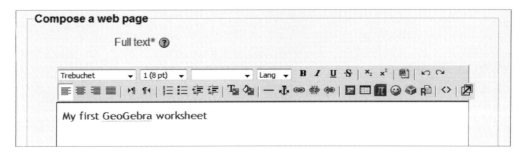

5. Select the text you've just entered, and click on the **Insert Web Link** button in the HTML editor's toolbar:

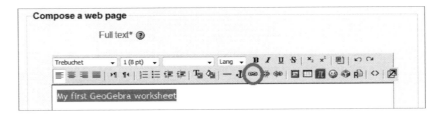

6. In the **Insert Link** dialog, click on the **Browse...** button. This takes you to your course files area. We need to upload and choose a GeoGebra file. I'm going to create a new folder for GeoGebra files and upload the file I created earlier in this chapter:

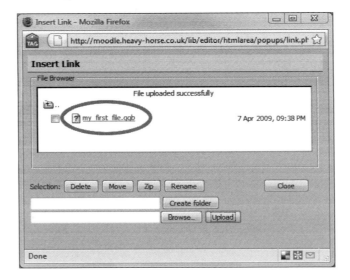

7. We have linked to the GeoGebra file, but without the GeoGebra filter students will be able to open it only if they have GeoGebra installed on their computer. Scroll to the bottom of the page and click on the **Save and display** button.

8. Moodle will try and display the GeoGebra worksheet. If you see a security warning, then click on the **Run** button. You may also see a message asking you to upgrade to the latest version of GeoGebra, but don't worry. It will all work the same.

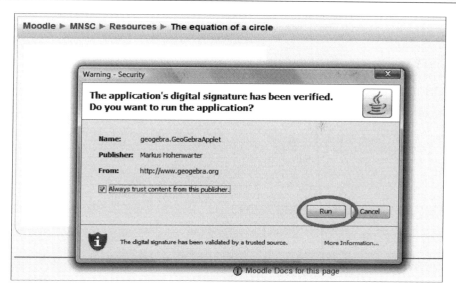

9. That's it! We can now incorporate GeoGebra worksheets in our Moodle courses:

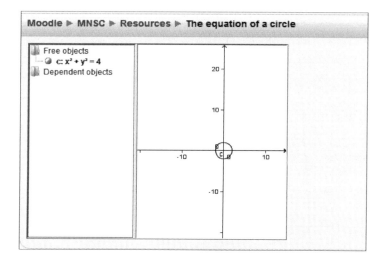

We've just seen how easy it is to incorporate GeoGebra worksheets in our Moodle courses using the GeoGebra filter. Using the filter means we don't have to rely on our students having GeoGebra installed on their computers (which, unless they are very keen, they probably won't).

Changing the size of the GeoGebra window

Do you need to make the GeoGebra window larger? Remember the files we copied over to our Moodle server? You'll find the settings you need in `filter.php`. The height and width settings in `filter.php` give the default values. It is possible to give a different height and width for each window. At the end of the link text, specify values for the width and height of the applet according to the following pattern:

```
myfile.ggbwidth=600height=300
```

(The default values are 400x400. Note that there is no space before 'width'.)

Interactive activities with GeoGebra—dynamic worksheets

So far, we've been creating static worksheets (for example, simply plotting functions for our students to view). I really want my students to start exploring mathematics in a more hands-on way, and GeoGebra's dynamic worksheets are a great way of doing that. Let's spend the next couple of sections exploring them.

Simple dynamic worksheets—Exploring linear functions with GeoGebra

Now let's see how we can create a simple interactive activity—a so-called dynamic worksheet—using GeoGebra. We'll start with an activity that allows our students to explore linear functions. The general equation of a straight line is this:

$$y=mx+c$$

Here, m is the gradient and c is the y intercept. I'm going to show you how to create an activity that allows your students to explore what happens when you vary m and c:

1. First, we need to create a new, empty worksheet in GeoGebra. Then, we need to specify the variables for m and c. Let's do that using sliders. Click on the slider button in GeoGebra's toolbar and select **Slider** from the drop-down menu. Note that you may have to click on the little arrow on the button—not just the button—to get the display below:

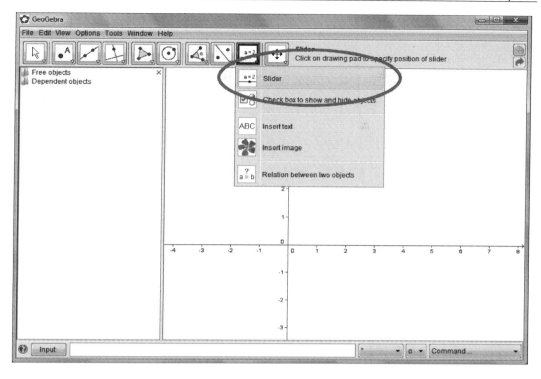

2. Click anywhere on the graphics view to add a slider (you can always move it later). In the **Slider** configuration dialog, call the variable **c** and specify the range:

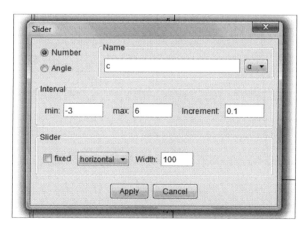

3. Repeat the process for **m** (the gradient). You should now have two sliders on the graphics view and two variables listed in the algebra view:

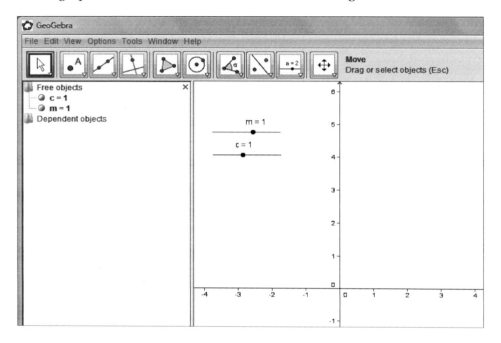

4. Now we specify the equation of a straight line, which will include the two new variables, m and c, we just specified:

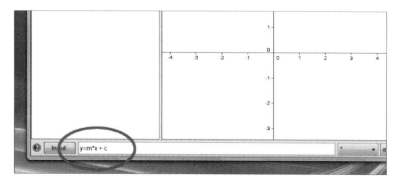

5. The line is now drawn on the graph. Moving the sliders changes the gradient and the y intercept. Note that you will need to click on the arrow button (on the far left of the toolbar) before you can actually move the sliders (if the slider button is still active on the toolbar, then you'll simply add more sliders to the graphics view!):

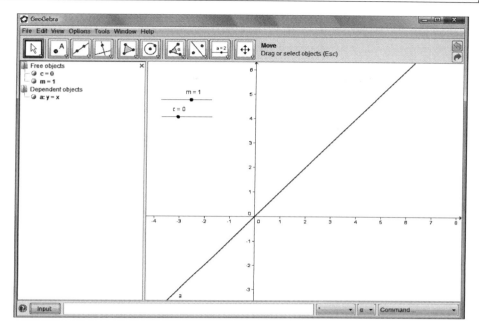

6. After reading the free GeoGebra book available from `http://www.geogebra.org/book/intro-en/` (which I don't really want to repeat here), I've rearranged the sliders, added some guidance text, and included the worksheet in a Moodle web page using the GeoGebra filter:

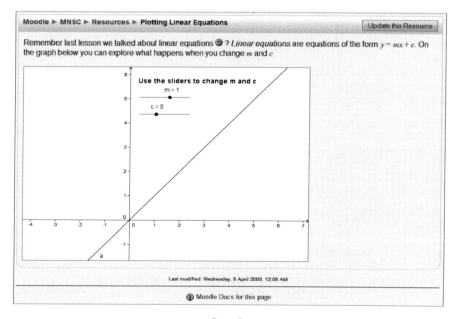

Advanced dynamic worksheets

We've seen how we can specify variables in GeoGebra and use sliders to allow our students to manipulate those variables. You can see how this provides us with a great way for students to explore complex mathematical subjects.

To that end, and with the skills we have just learned, let's now move on to the more complicated example—the Pythagorean Theorem.

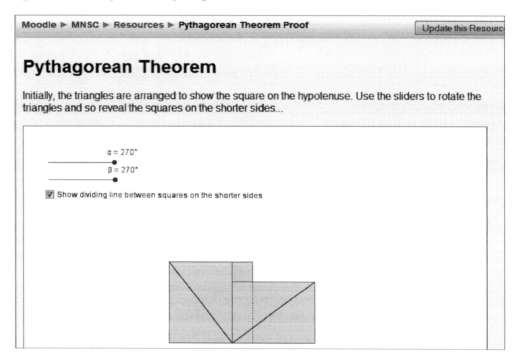

Exploring the Pythagorean Theorem with GeoGebra

In this example, I'm going to explore the relationship between the square on the hypotenuse and the sum of the squares on the other two sides:

1. In GeoGebra, create a new, empty worksheet. Right-click on the graph view, and select **Grid** from the menu. These grid lines will help us to construct a square of right-angled triangles.

2. From the main toolbar, select the **Polygon** tool. Again, you may need to click on the tiny arrow on the button, as well as the button itself, to see the screen below:

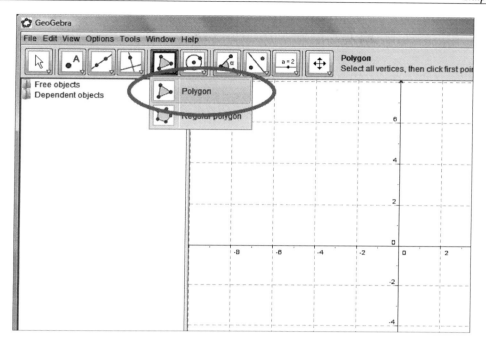

3. Use the Polygon tool to add a 3,4,5 triangle to the graphics view:

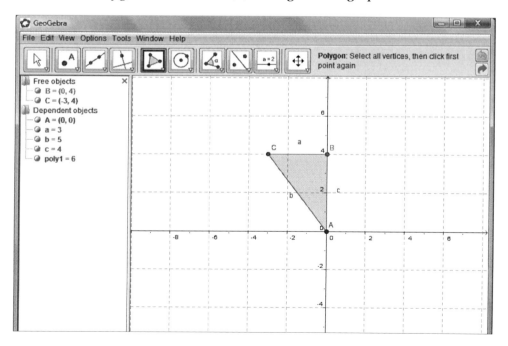

4. Repeat this process three more times to form a square:

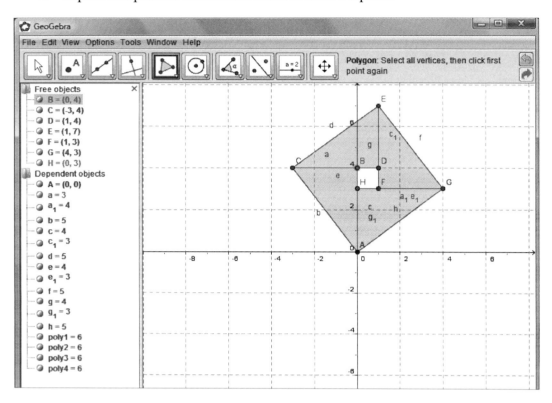

5. Next, we need to allow our students to rotate two of the triangles to form rectangles. Let's allow them to first rotate triangle CDE counterclockwise to form a rectangle with triangle ABC. First, let's add in a slider to allow the student to rotate the triangle from 0 to 270 degrees counterclockwise. Add a slider (using the slider option from the main toolbar), and configure the slider accordingly:

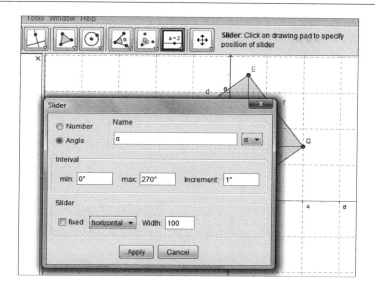

6. Click on the **Apply** button. Now select the **Rotate object around point by angle** tool:

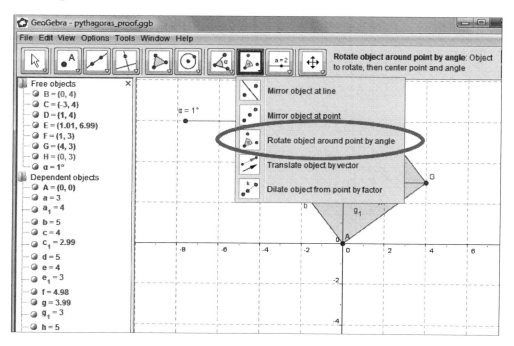

7. Select triangle CDE by clicking on it (the triangle will be highlighted when you hover the mouse pointer over it), and then click on point C. The **Rotate object around point by angle** configuration dialog will be displayed. Delete the angle in the text box and specify α from the drop-down list. This will allow us to use the slider to rotate the triangle:

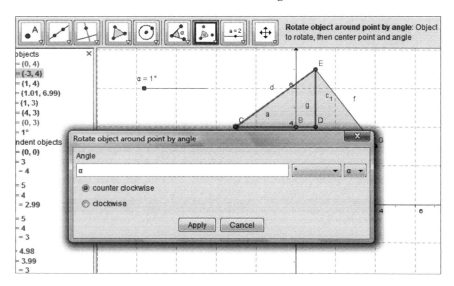

8. A new triangle has been added to the graph view. Click on the **Move** button in the main toolbar toolbar (the crosshairs arrow button), and try moving the slider to check that the triangle moves the right way within the correct limits. Remember that you might need to click on the tiny arrow before you see the crosshairs:

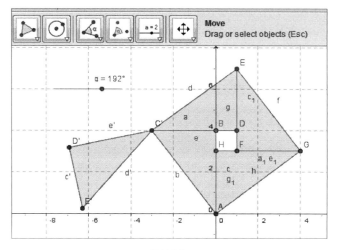

9. Repeat the process for triangle EFG. Remember that this triangle will now be rotating clockwise:

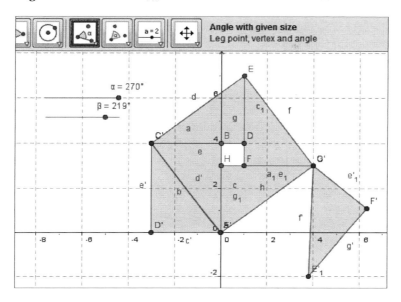

10. I'm now going to fill in the small square in the middle so that the proof looks more obvious:

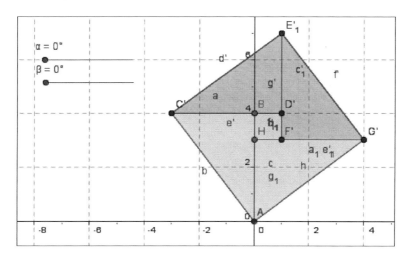

11. Now, we will delete triangles CDE and EFG because we don't need them anymore. I'm also going to remove the axes, grid lines, and hide the labels to tidy the graph view. To hide a label, right-click on the object listed under **Dependent objects** in the algebra view. Toggle the label's visibility using the **Show label** menu option:

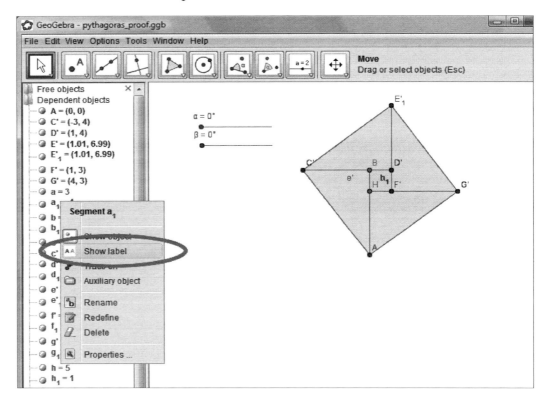

12. After hiding labels and with a little more rearranging, my GeoGebra worksheet is now ready to include in my Moodle course:

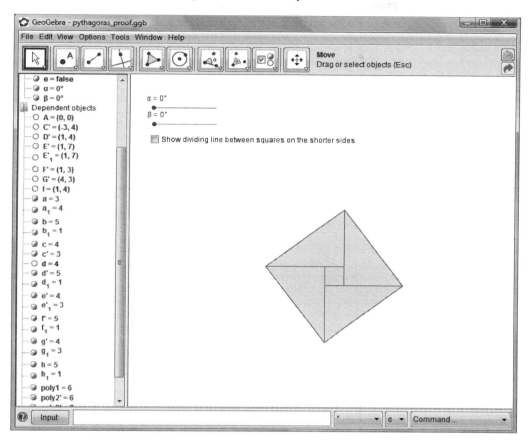

Exploring the Pythagorean Theorem with GeoGebra—recap

We have created a dynamic GeoGebra worksheet that allows our students to explore a proof of the Pythagorean Theorem. Now we just need to include the GeoGebra file in our Moodle courses. I've already got the GeoGebra filter installed, so including the proof is simple (see the *Installing the GeoGebra filter* section). Here it is included in a Moodle web page:

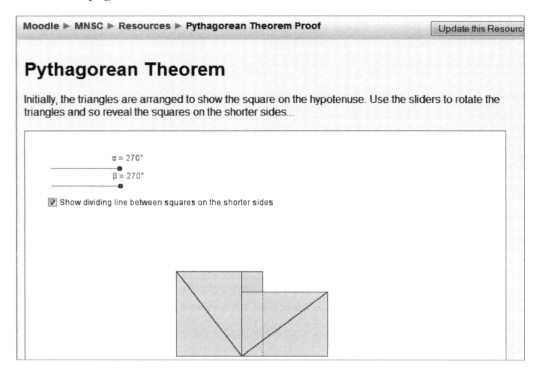

Hiding objects in the Graphics view

You probably noticed in the previous screenshot that I've included a checkbox that reveals a line segment—a line that divides the squares on the shorter two sides of the right-angled triangle. Can you find the menu option that allows you to do this?

Hint:
Check out the drop-down menu containing the Slider option.

More GeoGebra examples

GeoGebra provides our students with some great opportunities to explore mathematical relationships. There are some interesting examples (from both mathematics and science) on the GeoGebra Wiki. Here are just a few ideas:

- Create graphs of functions quickly. GeoGebra will allow your students to manipulate those graphs to explore relationships between variables.

- Use GeoGebra dynamic worksheets to explore visually mathematical concepts that are hard to explain in words (for example, simple harmonic motion).

- GeoGebra also supports derivatives; see the free online book *Introduction to GeoGebra* (`http://www.geogebra.org/book/intro-en/`) for more details.

- For more examples and samples you can download and experiment with yourself, check out the GeoGebra Wiki at `http://www.geogebra.org/en/wiki/`.

GeoGebra: Where to get further help

If you do find yourself needing help with a particular task, then there are two free online books available: *Introduction to GeoGebra* (`http://www.geogebra.org/book/intro-en/`) and the full *GeoGebra Manual* (`http://www.geogebra.org/help/docuen`).

Also, check out the GeoGebra User Forum at `http://www.geogebra.org/forum/`.

Summary

We've covered a great amount of work in this chapter. We saw how Moodle can be used to allow our students to explore complex geometric concepts in a truly hands-on way using the GeoGebra tool. We also learned that using the GeoGebra filter means we can integrate activities developed in GeoGebra in an almost seamless way. Specifically, we covered the following:

- How to install and use GeoGebra, the idea of a GeoGebra worksheet, and how to include one in a Moodle course
- The difference between static and dynamic worksheets and how to create both
- How to create a powerful, interactive proof of the Pythagorean Theorem

We've spent a good deal of time making our courses interactive and engaging, and so far we have been doing all the work. My students now need to start exercising their understanding of the Pythagorean Theorem. Let's learn how to create a Moodle quiz emphasizing question types that are especially useful in mathematics teaching.

6
Math Quizzes

Tired of marking all of those math tests you've set for your students? No problem! Now we can have Moodle do all of the grading for us! Getting to grips with the Pythagorean Theorem is going to take practice, and the Moodle Quiz module is going to give my students that practice without my having to worry about a mountain of marking. We'll see in this chapter that the Moodle Quiz module is a very powerful tool that not only automatically marks the answers for us, but also copes with different units (for example, answers given in feet or inches, meters or centimeters). We can also specify placeholders in the question that Moodle will replace with random numbers. This means we can provide lots of practice questions, which Moodle will both generate and mark automatically. Specifically, we will learn how to do the following:

- Create a math quiz and learn all about the different question types Moodle supports

- Install and use the feedback activity (not part of a normal Moodle install)

As good as the Moodle quiz module is at recognizing the correctness of our students' answers, we quickly run into problems when we need Moodle to recognize, for example, that $3a+2b$ is exactly the same as $2b+3a$. To accomplish this, we're going to need a **Computer Algebra System (CAS)**. The Maxima system (more on this later) has been successfully integrated into Moodle, thanks to the work carried out by Chris Sangwin and Alex Billingsley at the University of Birmingham in the UK. In this chapter, we will also learn how to perform these tasks:

- Install and integrate STACK into Moodle

- Create questions that can be automatically marked using STACK

Let's start by adding numeric questions into the course question bank.

Creating quizzes

Creating a quiz in Moodle is a two-stage process. First, we add our questions to the question bank (each course has its own question bank). Once we've added questions to the question bank, we can add a quiz activity to the course and then choose questions to add to it from the question bank. What are the advantages of having a two-stage process? I worked in much the same way creating quizzes before I started with Moodle. My bookshelf of math books was my question bank, and I would take questions from there to add into my quizzes. Here are just a few of the advantages:

- If there is a particular point you want to reinforce, then it's easy to include the same question in different quizzes throughout your course.

- It's easy to share your questions with other Moodle courses. For example, questions on the Pythagorean Theorem are relevant to pure math, mechanics, engineering, and physics.

- Questions can be exported from and imported into the question bank. This means converting questions over to Moodle is a job that can be shared between colleagues.

Here's a basic Pythagorean Theorem question I converted over to Moodle:

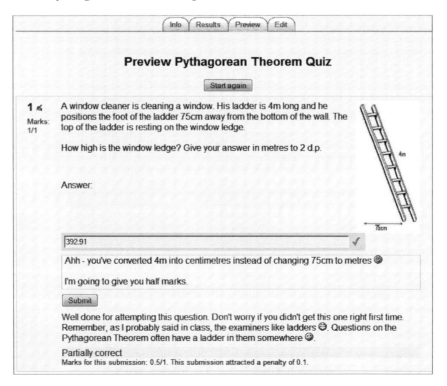

Question types

However, I don't want to convert just this single question over to Moodle;
I also want to have questions similar to this one but with different numbers.
I want those numbers chosen randomly by Moodle, so I don't have to keep thinking
up different numbers each time I set the quiz.

The question type I need is Calculated, which we'll learn about in the next section.

Calculated question type

Let's learn how to add a calculated question to the course question bank now:

1. Return to your course's front page, and click on **Questions** in the course
    Administration block:

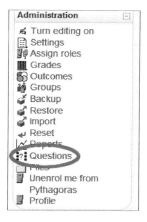

2. The course **Question bank** is displayed. From the **Create new question** drop-down menu, choose **Calculated**:

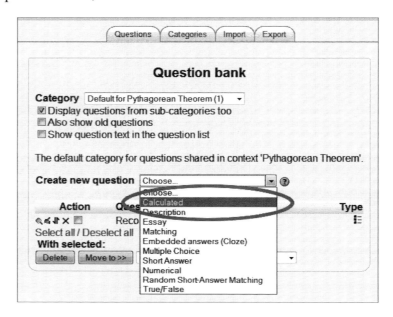

3. Give the question a name. Make sure it's a name that you (and, potentially, your colleagues) can recognize when it's in the question bank. Don't call it '1', 'i', or 'a)' because you don't know where it will appear in the quiz. Now, supply the question text:

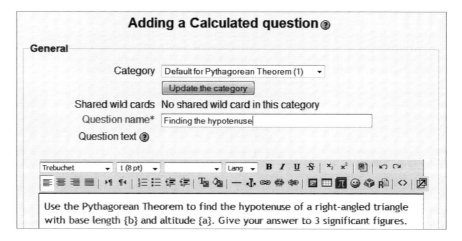

4. Notice that I have used placeholders in the text, {a} and {b}. We will be configuring Moodle to replace those with numbers shortly.

5. Scroll down to the **Answer** box. We need to enter the correct calculation into the **Correct Answer Formula** edit box (don't include a '=' in your answer):

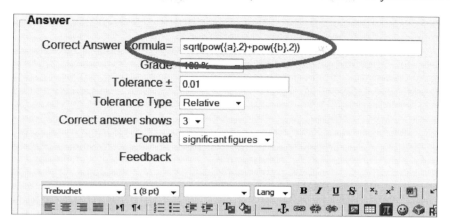

6. The students need to give the correct answer (exactly), but don't worry about the **Tolerance** setting: leave it set to **0.01**. Set the **Grade** to **100%**.

7. I want the students to give their answers to three significant figures, and to that end I needed to click on the **Correct answer shows** drop-down menu, set that to **3**, and change the **Format** to **significant figures**:

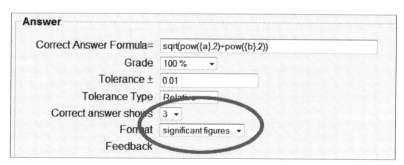

8. Scroll down to the bottom of the page, and click on the **Next Page** button. You are now taken to the **Choose dataset properties** page.

9. The numbers for the variables {a} and {b} will be chosen from a dataset. I want to use my own datasets for each variable. Select **will use a new shared dataset** for both drop-downs:

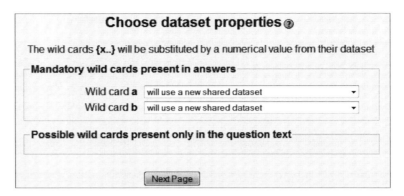

10. Click on the **Next Page** button. You are taken to the **Edit the datasets** page. Now, we can specify the range of values for {a} and {b}:

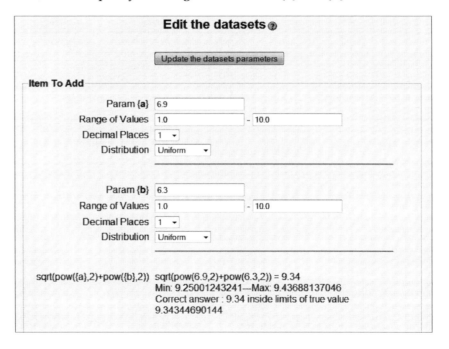

11. We need to add numbers to this dataset. I want to add 20 possible pairs of numbers for {a} and {b}. Scroll down to the **Add** box, select **20** items from the **item(s)** drop-down menu and click on the **Add** button:

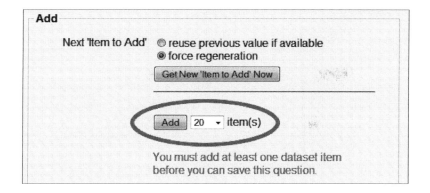

12. Twenty pairs of numbers are now added to the dataset. Moodle will choose pairs of numbers in this dataset when the student is presented with the question. If you want to alter any of the numbers Moodle has automatically generated for us, you can do so in the second-half of the page. Scroll down to the very bottom of the page, and click on the **Save changes** button.

13. Our new calculated question is now added to the question bank:

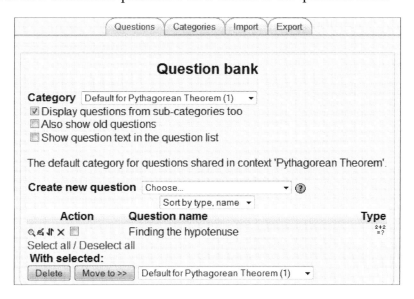

To recap, we have seen that creating a calculated question is a two-step process. First, we need to specify the question text. The question text contains variables that Moodle will then replace with random values when the quiz is taken. Then, we need to specify datasets for each of the variables, from which Moodle will choose the values when the quiz is taken. We can have Moodle choose the numbers for us, or we can select our own.

Including an image in the question text

Make your questions more engaging by including an image in the question text. Use the **Insert Image** button:

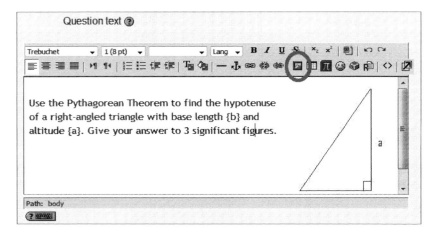

You can also include the image by using the **Image to display** drop-down menu:

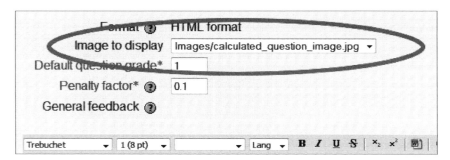

Calculated question type: Frequently asked questions

The calculated question type is extremely powerful, which means some settings can seem a little confusing. Below you'll find answers to just a few of the common queries regarding calculated questions:

- What math functions does the correct answer formula support? Notice that in my Pythagoras example, I squared the base and altitude using the `pow()` function, and I found the square root using the `sqrt()` function. For a full list of supported functions, check out `http://docs.moodle.org/en/question/type/calculated`.

- How do I specify alternative units? Imagine you have a question that accepts the answer in either centimeters or meters. The calculated question type allows us to accept answers in either unit:

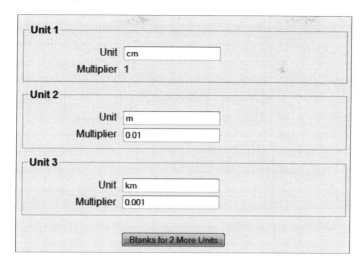

- What does it mean if a variable is listed under "Possible wild cards present only in the question text"? If your question contained text, which looked like a variable, or if you included a variable that isn't used in the correct answer formula, then these are listed on the **Choose dataset properties** page:

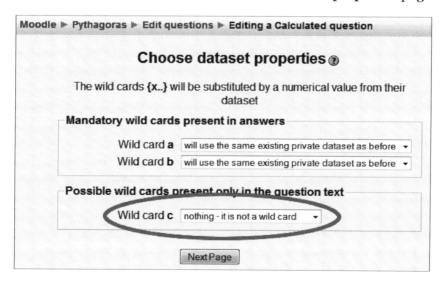

Numerical question type

Simpler to configure than a calculated question, but slightly less powerful, the numerical question type allows us to specify a correct answer along with a tolerance (or accepted error), so that answers within an accepted range are allowed. Let's take a look at another Pythagorean Theorem question I'm creating:

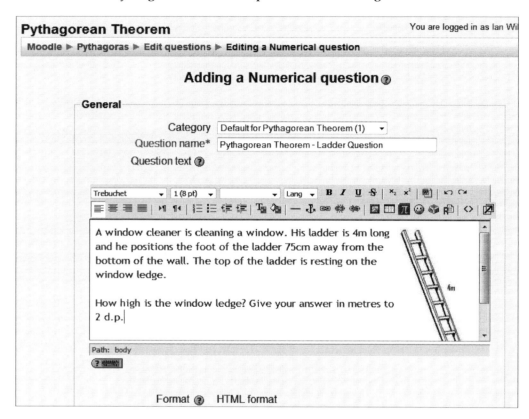

You can see that I've mixed units: the distance from the bottom of the ladder to the foot of the wall is measured in centimeters, and the length of the ladder is given in meters. The question specifies that you must give your answer in meters. However, I'm going to give half marks to students who give their answer in centimeters:

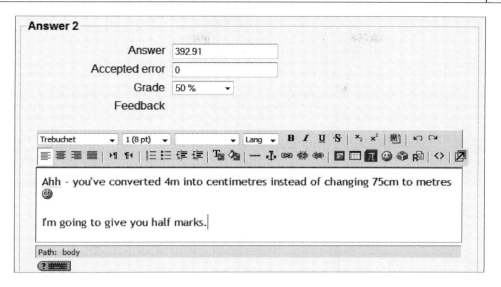

You can also catch the wrong answers:

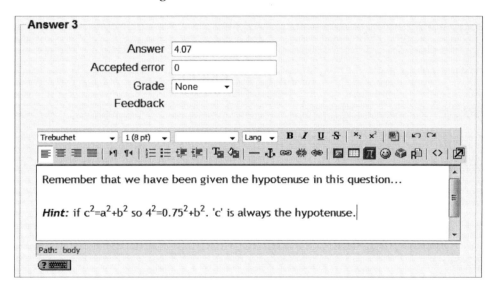

Additionally, you can keep track of any other possible wrong answer using "*":

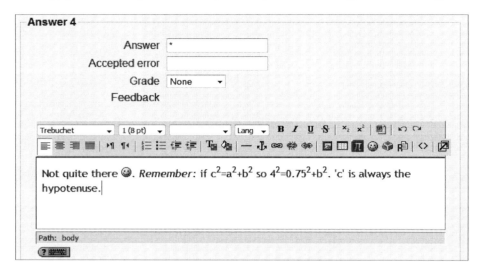

As with the calculated question type, scroll down to the bottom of the page and specify unit multipliers, if you wish.

Note that I've started providing some feedback. There's more on feedback later on in this chapter.

Other question types

In the previous section, we investigated two question types specifically designed to support numeric/mathematical questions. You must have also seen that there is a full range of selection and supply-type questions we can add into the question bank:

- **Multiple Choice**: Students select their answer from the available options. There are, in fact, two types of multiple choice questions: single answer and multiple answers (`http://docs.moodle.org/en/question/type/multichoice`).

- **Short-Answer**: Students respond with a word or phrase. You will need to specify the correct answers using wild cards, so that Moodle can pick the correct answers out of the responses students have typed. Take a look at Moodle docs for more information (`http://docs.moodle.org/en/question/type/shortanswer`).

- **Description**: This is not actually a question but a way of breaking up questions—perhaps providing some text/graphics or maybe a video presentation before a student attempts a set of questions.

- **Essay**: The student's answer is in essay format. If you are setting your students an assignment, then Moodle already has an 'assignment' activity specifically designed for this purpose. See `http://docs.moodle.org/en/question/type/essay`.

- **Matching**: The student is presented with questions, each of which has a drop-down list of possible answers. The student must match the correct answer to each question. For more details, see `http://docs.moodle.org/en/question/type/match`.

- **Random Short-Answer Matching**: You can choose how many 'sub-questions' are chosen (randomly) from the short-answer questions that are available. See `http://docs.moodle.org/en/question/type/randomsamatch` for details.

- **Embedded Answers (Cloze)**: This is a fill-the-gaps exercise greatly enhanced by virtue of being "computerized". Moodle presents the user with a passage of text that has questions embedded in it. The correct answers complete the text (see `http://docs.moodle.org/en/question/type/multianswer`).

- **Random**: This is a completely random question chosen by Moodle.

Import your questions: Hot Potatoes quiz

Are you a Hot Potatoes user? If so, then you can import your Hot Potatoes quiz into your course question bank. With the question bank page open, click on the **Import** tab. Follow the instructions to import a Hot Potatoes quiz:

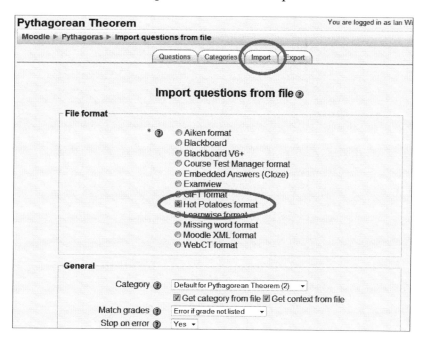

Note that you can't import all Hot Potatoes question types (there is no equivalent to the Hot Potatoes crossword question in Moodle, for instance). Also, it's the Hot Potatoes project file you need to import, rather than creating a web page.

Now that we've added questions to the question bank, let's see how to get those questions included in a quiz.

Adding a math quiz

Once we've added a question or two to the question bank, we can add a quiz to our course. I want a simple quiz where each student is allowed one attempt with no help along the way. Let's see how to achieve this now:

1. Return to your course's front page, choose a topic, click on the **Add an activity** drop-down menu, and select **Quiz** from the list.

2. Give the quiz a name (this will appear on the course's front page) and, if you wish, you can specify a short introduction:

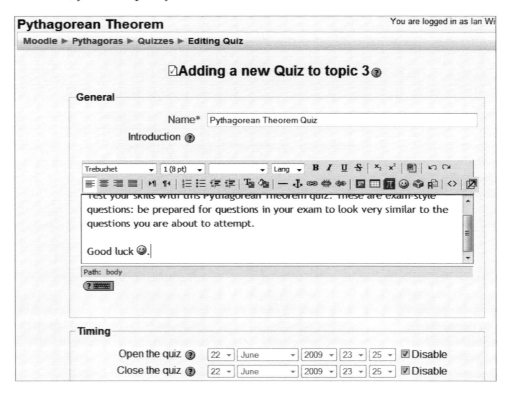

3. Scroll down to the **Attempts** box. Set **Attempts allowed** to **1** and **Adaptive mode** to **No**:

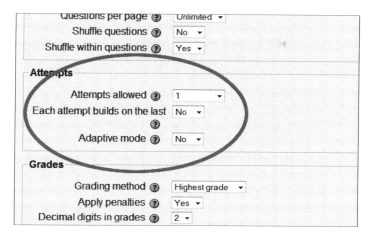

4. Scroll down to the bottom of the page, and click the **Save and display** button. A split screen page is displayed with the course question bank on the right and the (currently empty) quiz on the left:

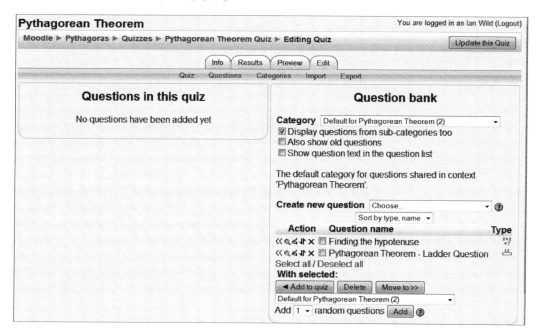

5. To add questions from the question bank to the quiz, simply select them and click on the **Add to quiz** button:

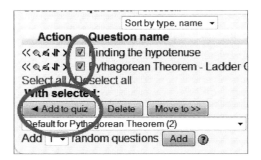

6. The questions are now added to the quiz. You'll now see them listed on the left-hand side of the page:

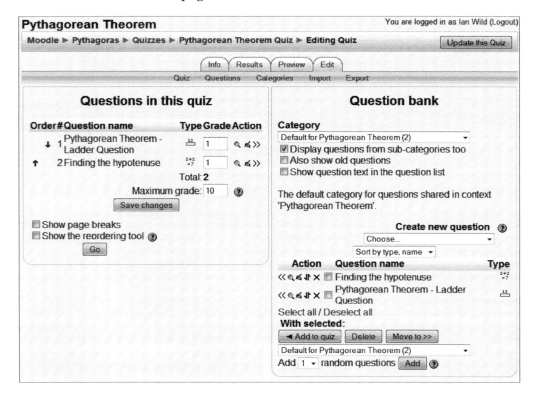

7. To preview the quiz, click on the **Preview** tab at the top of the page:

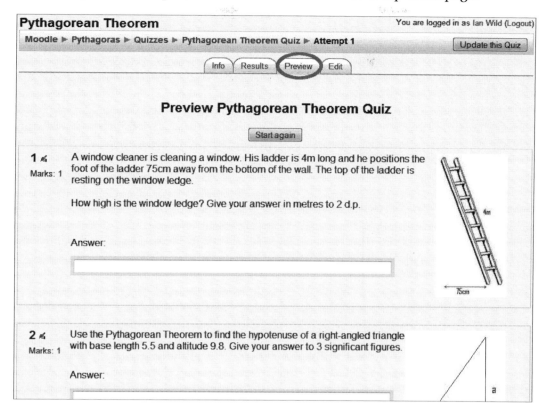

8. That's it! The quiz is now configured.

Recall that I set **Adaptive mode** to **No**. Adaptive mode adds a **Submit** button to each question, allowing students (with some suitable feedback from me) to learn from their mistakes as they work through the quiz. Try experimenting with this setting. See how your students behave with the **Submit** button. For example, don't let them think that they can guess a multiple choice answer until they eventually get it right. Remind them that they'll be penalized for each wrong answer.

Encouraging students as they attempt the quiz

You've seen that there are a lot of settings I've simply ignored as I've configured this quiz. Return to your course's front page, and click on **Questions** from the course administration block to open the course **Question bank**. Click on the edit icon next to the numerical question we configured earlier in this chapter. (Have you spotted that you can tell what type of question it is from the icon on the far-right? Hover the mouse pointer over the icon.):

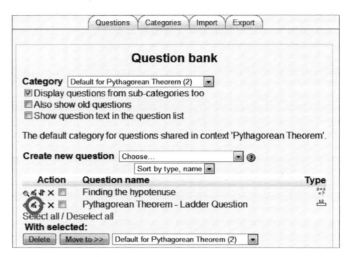

Remember how I mentioned that I'd started filling out feedback? I'm going to finish doing that now in this question by giving some **General feedback**:

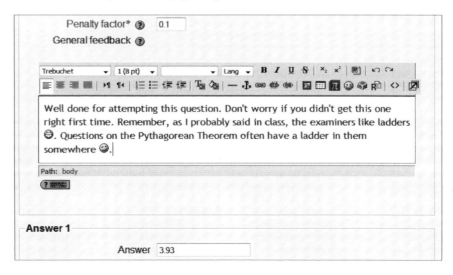

When you are happy with your feedback, remember to scroll to the bottom of the page and click on the **Save changes** button. Now, return to your course's front page, turn editing on, and click on the update icon next to the quiz we added in the previous section:

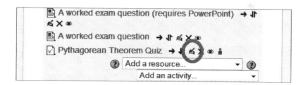

On the quiz configuration page, scroll down to the **Attempts** section and set **Adaptive mode** to **Yes**:

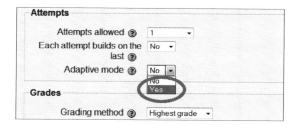

Scroll to the bottom of the page, and click on the **Save changes** button.

Preview the quiz now, and notice that under each question there is a **Submit** button. Experiment with entering both correct and incorrect responses. Click on the **Submit** button, and see how Moodle reacts by giving the student our feedback. Remember: if you are planning to use **Adaptive mode**, then it's worth reminding your students that they will be penalized if they get an answer wrong!

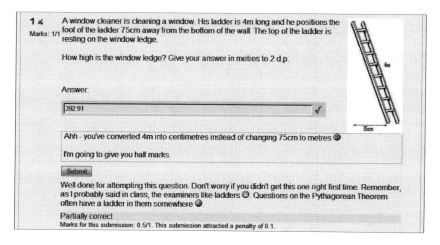

Reporting quiz results

What's great about a Moodle quiz is the detailed reporting Moodle provides for us. Here is an example of the report page for my quiz once a student has attempted it. (In fact, this is a colleague of mine helping me to check that my feedback is understandable!):

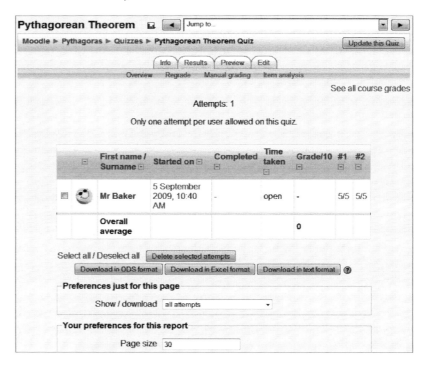

Such reporting not only allows us to see what our students have been up to, but I also find it an invaluable tool for determining the success of my teaching.

 Once someone has attempted your quiz, you can no longer modify it (add or remove questions). You will need to delete the attempts to unlock the quiz.

Monitoring the success of your teaching

Having a course question bank means it's easy for me to reuse questions. I often start and end a Moodle course with a short quiz (the same questions before they start and after they have completed the course). I need to check that they don't know less than when they started!

The Feedback module

We ended the previous section thinking about how to use a Moodle quiz to monitor the success of your teaching. You can indeed use a Moodle quiz to gather this kind of data if you wish for feedback or perhaps even for a data handling exercise. For example, the Pythagorean Theorem is used by builders to ensure that each corner of a room is a right-angle. I've asked my students to measure the lengths of a room at home, and we'll check in class to see if the corner of the room is, in fact, a right-angle!

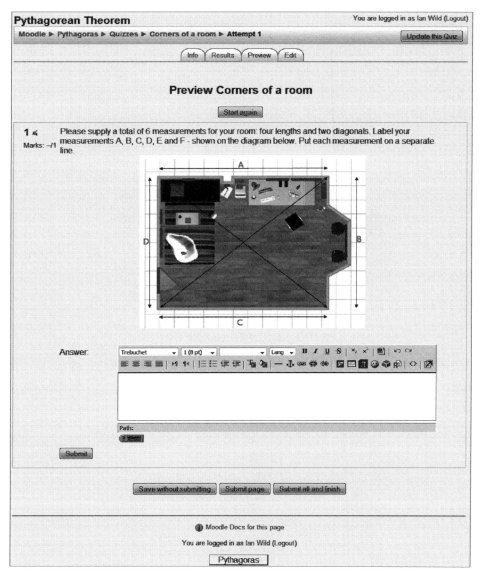

In the previous screenshot, you can see a preview of the essay question I initially used to gather that data. The main problem with using a Moodle quiz to gather data is that it isn't really the right tool for the job. The answers to the quiz questions are either right, wrong, or somewhere in between, and this doesn't apply if we simply want to gather data. So, rather than using a quiz to gather this information, I've asked my Moodle administrator to install the Feedback module.

Check out the *Ask the admin* section at the end of this chapter for more information on getting the Feedback module installed on your system.

Gathering Feedback

Let's see how easy it is to use the Feedback module to gather data from our students.

Configuring a Feedback activity

The first step is to add a feedback activity to our courses. Then, we need to configure it:

1. Return to your course's front page, turn on the editing, choose a topic, click on the **Add an activity** drop-down menu, and select **Feedback** from the list:

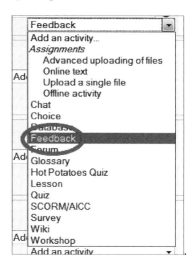

2. Give your new feedback activity a name and provide a description:

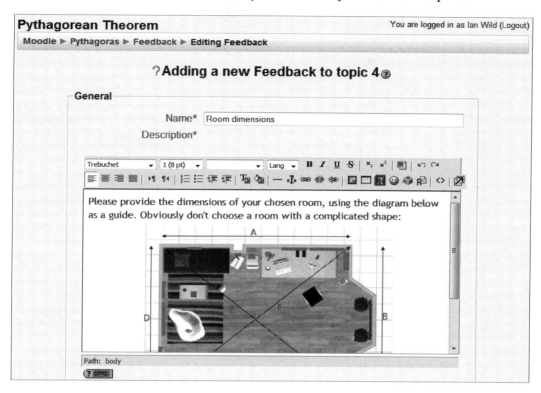

3. Now, select your feedback options. I want to know who has supplied what data, so I'm going to **Record user names**:

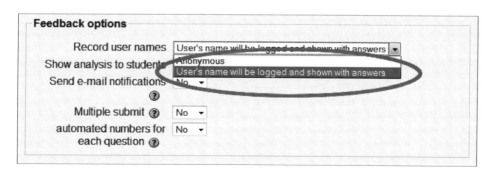

4. If you wish, you can provide extra information (or just a simple thank you) after a student has completed the feedback form:

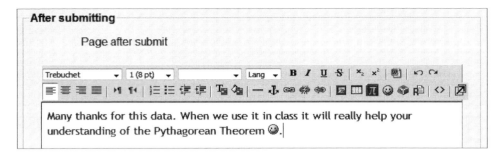

5. Scroll down to the bottom of the page, and click on the **Save and display** button. Click on the **Edit questions** tab at the top of the page:

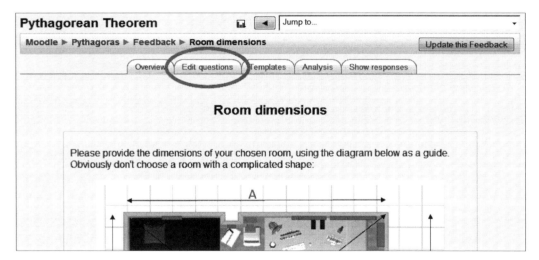

6. We can now start to add questions to the feedback form. I'm going to include six **Numeric answer** questions, asking for the lengths of A,B,C,D,E, and F to correspond with the labels in my room plan diagram. Select **Numeric answer** from the list of question types:

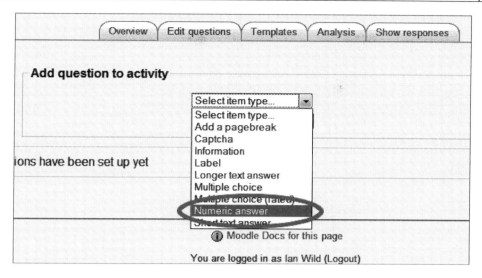

7. Complete the necessary options:

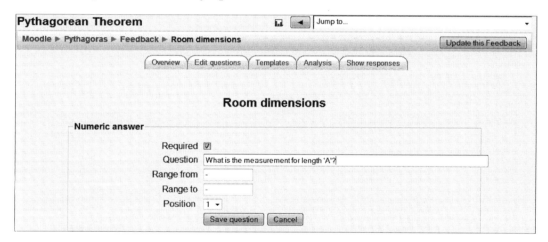

8. Repeat this process for each length:

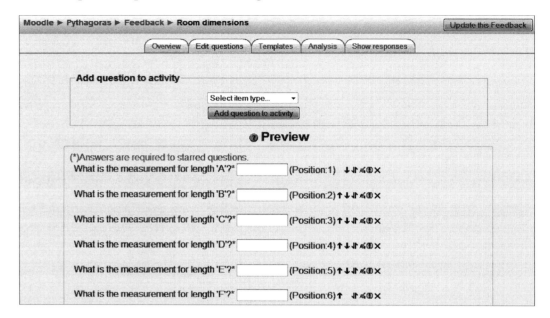

9. When you are finished, return to your course's front page using the breadcrumbs across the top of the page. And that's it! We're finished configuring the feedback form.

View your students' responses by clicking on the **Show Responses** tab. Note that under the **Analysis** tab, you've got the option to export responses to Excel (either to store them elsewhere or to analyze them further).

Feedback example: Create a departmental survey

Do you need to survey your students at the end of the academic year to see what they thought of your teaching? The Feedback module provides the ideal answer. Requesting feedback online means no more working your way through piles of paper.

 If you want to take a straw poll, then take a look at the Choice activity at http://docs.moodle.org/en/Choices.

System for Teaching and Assessment using a Computer algebra Kernel (STACK)

For my more advanced students, I have a set of Pythagorean Theorem questions where the lengths of sides are algebraic expressions, rather than just numbers. My students need to demonstrate their aptitude with quadratic expressions.

For example, they should be able to expand *(x+4)(x-3)*.

The solution to this problem is usually written as x^2+x-12. But what if the students entered $x-12+x^2$? Would Moodle still mark this answer as correct?

At the very least, we need a question type that understands the commutative, associative, and distributive properties. The solution is provided by a Computer Algebra System (CAS). For a general background on computer algebra systems, refer to http://en.wikipedia.org/wiki/Computer_algebra_system.

STACK is a Computer Aided Assessment (CAA) system that overcomes these kinds of mathematical problems. STACK is the brainchild of Chris Sangwin; for more details on STACK, check out the STACK documentation at http://stack.bham.ac.uk/wiki/index.php/Main_Page. For more information on the STACK philosophy, read http://stack.bham.ac.uk/wiki/index.php/The_philosophy_of_STACK.

In the next section, I will provide you with an introduction to STACK and demonstrate how to create a couple of basic questions.

System requirements

At the time of writing, STACK (version 2) requires the following two extra components to be installed on your server:

Server component	Web address	Description
Maxima	http://maxima.sourceforge.net/	The computer algebra system (CAS) used by STACK
GNUPLOT	http://www.gnuplot.info/	A data and function plotting utility

You will find full details on how to install both Maxima and GNUPLOT at the web addresses given in the table.

Moodle requirements

Ensure you have installed and enabled a Moodle filter for converting LaTeX to mathematical notation. This is covered in detail in Chapter 7. If you're still not sure, then check out both the Moodle docs (`http://docs.moodle.org/en/Mathematics`) and the Mathematics Tools forum (`http://moodle.org/mod/forum/view.php?id=752`) on moodle.org.

Part of the STACK installation process requires you to install a new question type. Don't worry! Everything you need is contained in the STACK distribution files.

Installing STACK

Once your server is configured correctly with all of the relevant software, then you will need to install STACK.

Rather than repeating what is eloquently described online, I'm going to refer you to `http://stack.bham.ac.uk/wiki/index.php/Installation`, where the process is described in detail.

Here's what you get once STACK is installed:

- A new block, allowing you to control the STACK system directly from Moodle:

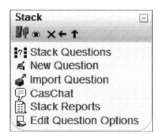

- A new question type, **Opaque**:

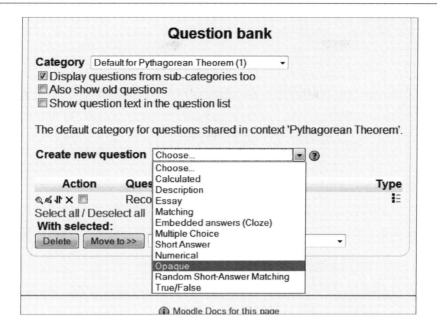

Let's learn how to create quiz questions using STACK.

Using STACK

My original problem was this: how can I ask my students to expand *(x+4)(x-3)* and have Moodle automatically mark my students' answers—hopefully with an answer equivalent to x^2+x-12. Let's create that question now.

Creating a STACK question

Return to your course's front page and, from the course administration block, click on **Questions** to open the course question bank. Then, follow these steps:

1. Click on the **Create new question** drop-down menu and choose **Opaque**:

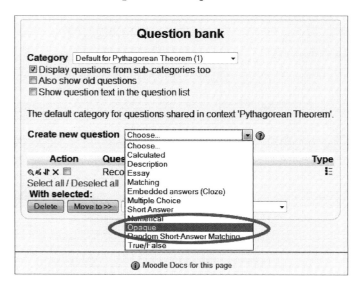

2. On the **Add Opaque Question** page, click on **Manage Stack Questions**:

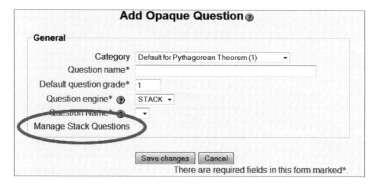

3. A new window (or tab, depending on your browser) is opened. On the
    Questions available from STACK question engine page, click on the
    New Question link:

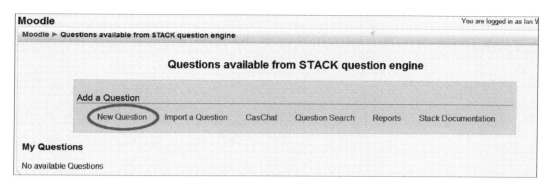

4. Give your question a name (suitable for you to be able to find it again and
    know what the question is when you do).

5. Write your question in the **Question Stem**. You need to be careful with the
    format: math notation can be written in LaTeX (denoted, in my case, with
    single dollars). Note how I've specified a variable for the student's answer
    (**#answer#**). You can call this variable whatever you like, as long as you
    enclose it in #:

Author a question on STACK

Name:	Expanding brackets question
Description:	
Keywords:	
Question Variables:	
Question Stem:	Expand $(x+4)(x-3)$. #answer#
#ans# denotes student answers @castext@ for castext <html></html> for html \latex for latex	
Worked Solution:	

6. Scroll down to the **Update** button immediately under the **Question Note** option and click on it:

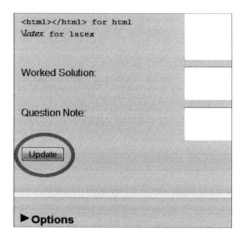

7. An **Interaction Elements** section is now inserted into the page. You will need to specify the answer in the **Teacher's Answer** row. Be careful with the format as it has to be a valid CAS expression (for example, 3x should be specified as 3*x). When you have filled in your answer, click on the **Update** button at the bottom of this section:

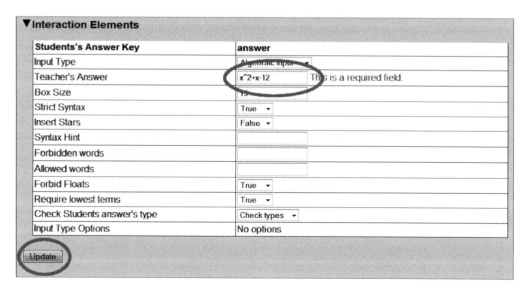

8. We've asked the question and specified our answer. We now need to program STACK to understand whether or not the student's answer is correct. In the **Potential Response Trees** block, specify a name for the response and press the **+** button:

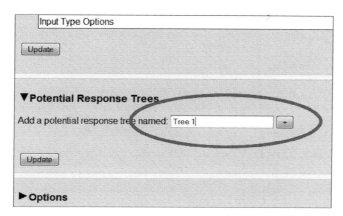

9. The student's answer is stored in the variable **answer**. My answer needs to be specified in the **TAns** (teacher's answer box). As this is the correct answer, I can copy and paste from the **Teacher's Answer** in the **Interaction Elements** box. Notice that the **Answer test** is **AlgEquiv** (algebraic equivalents):

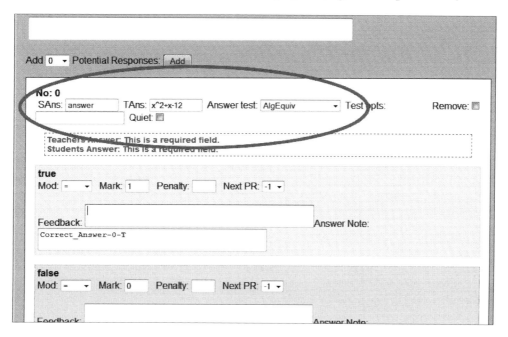

10. Now, click on the **Update** button at the bottom of the **Potential Response Trees** section.

11. A common mistake when expanding brackets is to forget to multiply out completely (typically submit x^2-12 as the answer). Let's accommodate this now in the **Potential Response Trees**. Add another PR (potential response) by choosing to add 1 new potential response from the drop-down list and clicking the **Add** button:

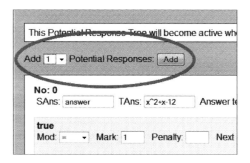

12. Populate the new potential response with the incorrect answer and some feedback. Remember to ensure that they aren't awarded a mark for getting the answer wrong:

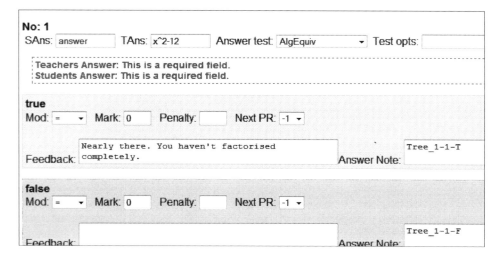

13. We now have two nodes in the Potential Response Trees that we need to link together. From the actual correct answer response (node **No: 0**), click on the **Next PR** drop-down in the **false** block and choose **1**:

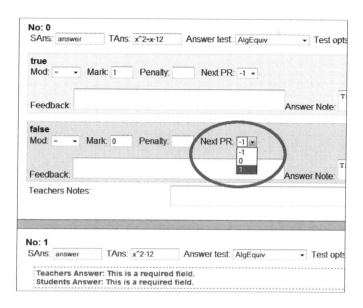

14. Can you see how we are linking potential responses together to form a tree of nodes? Click on the **Update** button at the bottom of the **Potential Responses** section to save your changes.

15. Scroll down to the bottom of the page, and click on the **Save** button:

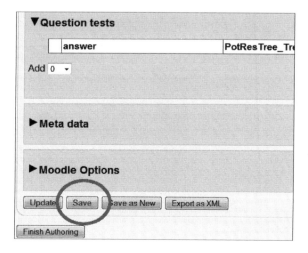

16. The page reloads, and if we have specified everything correctly, then we now have the opportunity to try our new question. Click on **Try question**:

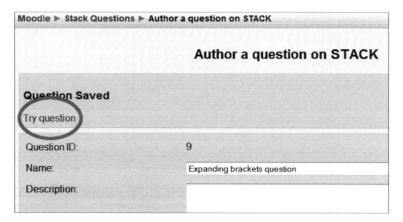

17. Try specifying different answers to see how Moodle responds. Make sure any feedback you specified is displayed correctly:

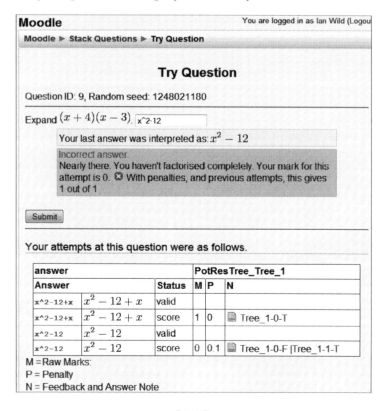

18. When you have finished testing, click on the **Finished** button at the bottom of the page.

19. The next step is to deploy the question in order for us to include it in a quiz. On the **Questions available from STACK question engine** page, click on the **Deploy** link:

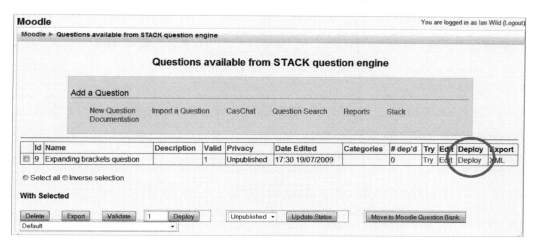

20. The question is now deployed:

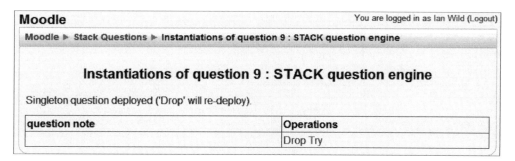

21. Close the STACK question configuration window (or tab, depending on your browser) and return to the **Add Opaque Question** page. Refresh the page in your browser. Our new question will be listed in the **Question Name** drop-down list. When you have your STACK question selected, give the Moodle question a name:

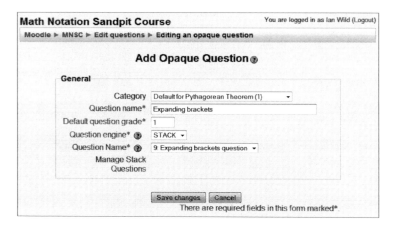

22. Save the changes by clicking on the **Save changes** button.

That's it! We're done.

We are now ready to add this question into a quiz. If you haven't read them already, you'll find the details on this process earlier in this chapter in the Adding a math quiz section. Here is how my question looks:

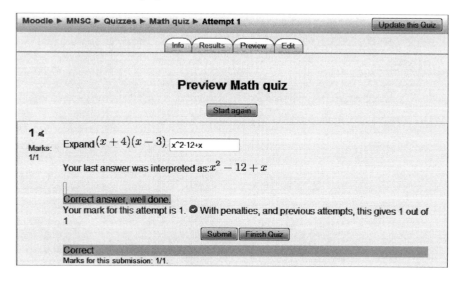

Enhancing STACK questions—graphs, charts, and random variables

Although not immediately obvious, you can certainly include images and graphs in your **Question Stem**. Here is an example of a Google chart included in the stem:

Question Stem:	`<p><img src="http://chart.apis.google.com/chart?`
	`chs=300x100`
`#ans#` denotes student answers	`&chd=t:5,15,4,3,3`
`@castext@` for castext	`&cht=p3`
`<html></html>` for html	`&chl=France (3)|UK (13)|Italy (1)|Spain (6)|USA (1)"`
`\latex` for latex	`alt="pie chart" /></p>`
	A school class were asked where they went on holiday last year. The results are shown in the pie chart. The numbers of students visiting each country is given in brackets. What percentage of students visited Spain?
	`#ans# <IEfeedback>ans</IEfeedback> <PRTfeedback>tree</PRTfeedback>`

Here's how it looks when included in a Moodle quiz:

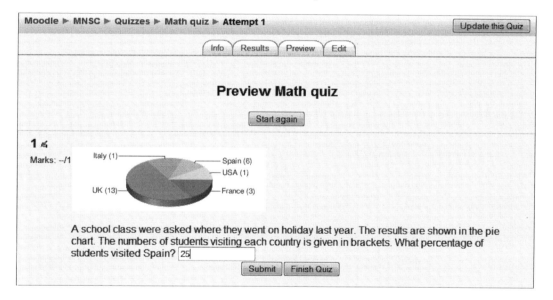

Remember that we needed to install GNUPLOT on the server. This is because we can also plot functions in the stem using special commands. Here's another example (from the STACK sample questions):

Name:	test_4
Description:	Plots in question, feedback and worked solution.
Keywords:	
Question Variables:	p = x^2
Question Stem: #ans# denotes student answers @castext@ for castext <html></html> for html \latex for latex	Below is a sketch of a graph. Find an algebraic expression which represents it. @plot(p,[x,-2,2])@ $f(x)=$#ans1#. <IEfeedback>ans1</IEfeedback> <PRTfeedback>plots</PRTfeedback>
Worked Solution:	The graph @plot(p,[x,-2,2])@ has algebraic expression [f(x)=@p@.]

This will be displayed as the following:

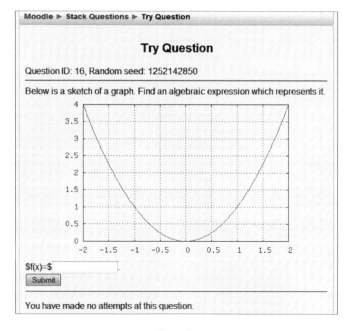

From this example, you can see how easy it is to include HTML in the stem text. For more details on what you can include in the stem, visit `http://stack.bham.ac.uk/wiki/index.php/CASText`.

You can also include random variables in your questions. Check out `http://stack.bham.ac.uk/wiki/index.php/Authoring_quick_start` for more information on random questions.

Getting more help with STACK

For extra help with STACK don't forget to check out the STACK Wiki at `http://stack.bham.ac.uk/wiki/index.php/Main_Page`. There is also a STACK Moodle at `http://www.stack.bham.ac.uk/` that is well worth visiting.

Ask the admin: Installing the Feedback module

Currently, the Feedback module is an optional module. You will need to visit `http://moodle.org/mod/data/view.php?d=13&rid=95` to download the correct package (depending on the version of Moodle you have installed). Let's run through the process:

1. Remember to enable **Maintenance mode** when installing new features into your Moodle. From the **Site Administration** block, select **Server | Maintenance mode**. You can also specify an optional maintenance message:

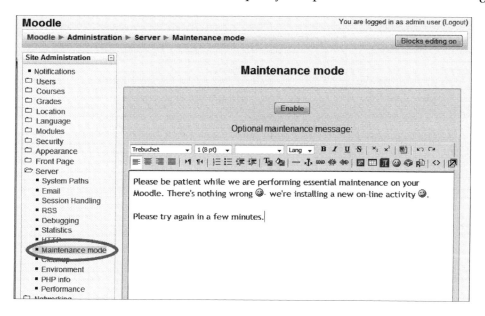

2. Once we have the correct package downloaded, we need to make sure the contents are extracted to the correct locations on the server. Obviously, how you get the files to where they need to be on your server depends on your system configuration. For example, if you are running your own server or if you are using shared hosting, you may want to download the package to your own computer and upload them to the server using an FTP client. In fact, I've downloaded the package directly to my Moodle server (a Linux server), and I'm going to extract them directly to the correct locations on the server using Unzip.

3. Once the files have been copied over, make sure file permissions and file ownership are set correctly.

4. Once the Feedback module files have been copied over, we need to return to the site' front page and click on **Notifications** in the **Site Administration** block:

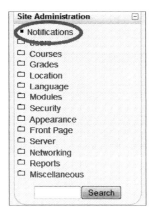

5. Moodle will now update its internal database, creating all the tables required for the new module. Because we are installing both a new activity and a new block, there are two sets of tables Moodle needs to configure. As Moodle configures its internal database, click on the **Continue** button when required:

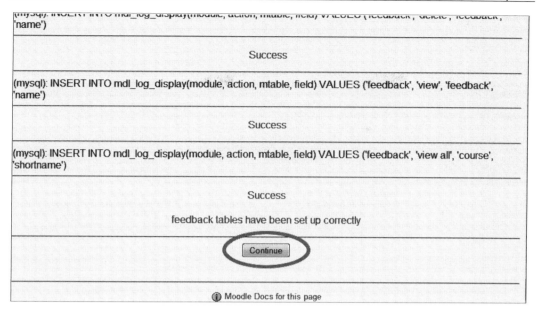

(mysql): INSERT INTO mdl_log_display(module, action, mtable, field) VALUES ('feedback', 'delete', 'feedback', 'name')

Success

(mysql): INSERT INTO mdl_log_display(module, action, mtable, field) VALUES ('feedback', 'view', 'feedback', 'name')

Success

(mysql): INSERT INTO mdl_log_display(module, action, mtable, field) VALUES ('feedback', 'view all', 'course', 'shortname')

Success

feedback tables have been set up correctly

Continue

Moodle Docs for this page

6. Once Moodle has finished configuring its internal database, visit any course and turn on the editing. Click on any **Add an activity** drop-down menu, and you will see that a new **Feedback** activity has been added to the list:

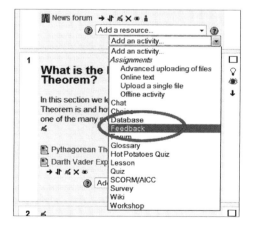

7. Likewise, click on the **Blocks** block, and you will see that a new **Feedback** block has been added to the list of available blocks:

 Did you remember to enable maintenance mode? We need to remember to disable it through the **Site Administration** block and the **Server | Maintenance mode** link.

The Feedback module is now ready to use.

Summary

In this chapter, we learned how to include math quizzes in our Moodle courses. Specifically, we covered these topics:

- How to create a Moodle quiz. We investigated both the calculated and numerical question types (extremely useful for math teaching).
- How to install and use the Feedback module.
- How to install and integrate STACK into Moodle.
- How to create algebra questions that can be automatically marked using STACK.

We saw how Moodle is great for creating and marking questions automatically. There is a potential problem with Moodle not being able to properly understand the commutative and associative properties (especially when it comes to algebraic structures), but we installed STACK to address this issue.

In the next chapter, we will be investigating math notation for further and higher education.

7
More Mathematical Notation

In Chapter 2, we investigated two ways of including mathematical notation in our Moodle courses. The first was to use third-party applications (Microsoft Office or OpenOffice.org) to generate the notation that we then copy into our courses. The second was to have the notation generated from within Moodle using a special filter—the Algebra Filter. In this chapter, we will investigate three more filters that you can use to generate mathematical notation:

- TeX
- jsMath
- ASCIIMathML

All three generate more advanced mathematical notation than can be achieved using the Algebra Filter. Both the TeX and jsMath filters use a special typesetting language called LaTeX (pronounced *lah-tek*), which we will be learning about in this chapter. However, ASCIIMathML doesn't use LaTeX. Also, it has the advantage that the notation it creates is far more accessible when displayed to the students even if they are blind or visually impaired.

At this stage you may be concerned that you will need to learn a whole new typesetting language (LaTeX) in order to include math notation in your course. Don't worry! We'll begin this chapter by showing you a Moodle module that adds an easy to use drag-and-drop equation generator to your HTML editor—DragMath.

In this chapter we shall look into the following:

- How to install and use the TeX and jsMath filters
- How to use DragMath, a fully integrated drag-and-drop equation editor
- How to produce fully accessible math notation using the ASCIIMathML filter
- The requirements of the Moodle server and our Internet browsers in order to support fully accessible mathematical notation

Why is including mathematical notation so complicated?

I've spent a portion of my career working in the newspaper business, at the time when movable type (letters and symbols on separate tiny blocks of metal, arranged by a typesetter) was being replaced by photographic film. In those distant 'movable type' days, creating mathematical notation was considered so special (and difficult) that typesetters used to charge extra to compose it. When we became computerized, arranging mathematical notation should have been easy, assuming the software used to compose the pages supported math notation. Unfortunately, the software often didn't! To solve the problem, Donald Knuth developed his own typesetting system called TeX, which was a formatting language not just for mathematics but for entire documents. It was Leslie Lamport who created LaTeX (again, pronounced *lah-tek*), a more advanced version of TeX, built on the same technology.

In order to produce mathematical notation, we can write an equation in the TeX language and have Moodle compose the math for us. We saw in Chapter 2 how the Algebra Filter produces mathematical notation. The problem with that filter is that you soon reach the limit of its abilities if you desire to compose anything more complicated than seventh grade (ages 11 to 14) mathematics.

Let's address this problem and turn on the TeX filter.

Advanced notation using the TeX filter

As we have seen, turning on the TeX filter means we can write mathematical notation in TeX and have Moodle convert this into formal mathematical notation for us. For example, `x=\frac{-b\pm\sqrt{b^2-4ac}}{2a}` is converted into this:

$$x = \frac{-b \pm \sqrt{b^2 - 4ac}}{2a}$$

Notice how we don't have to worry about the arrangement of the symbols; the filter will do all of that for us.

Turning on the TeX filter

Before we use the TeX filter, we need to make sure it is switched on. That means logging in to Moodle with administrator privileges. If you don't have these privileges then at this stage you'll need to hand this book over to your friendly Moodle admin:

1. Make sure you are logged into Moodle as an administrator. Find the **Site Administration** block on the site's front page. Select **Modules | Filters | Manage filters**:

2. On the **Manage filters** page, find the TeX filter in the list of installed filters, and make sure it's enabled:

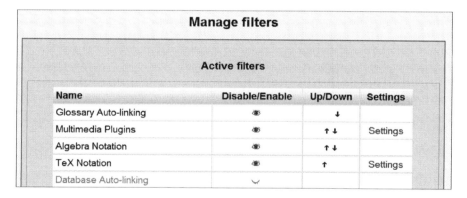

3. If it isn't enabled, then the eye will be closed. Poke the eye to enable it.

4. That's it! We're done.

We've just enabled the TeX filter. Remember that we've just enabled a "filter" that will filter out TeX math notation in any text we add to our Moodle course. (It will not filter separate documents/presentations/handouts that we upload. Moodle isn't that clever.) Let's now test the TeX filter to ensure it is behaving as it should.

Testing the TeX filter

In Chapter 2, we tried testing the Algebra Filter by including a simple fraction in our course. Now that we've turned on the TeX filter, let's try to include the algebraic representation of the Pythagorean Theorem:

1. Go to your course's front page. Turn on the editing, click on the **Add a resource** drop-down menu, and select **Compose a web page** from the list. Try typing the following into the HTML editor:

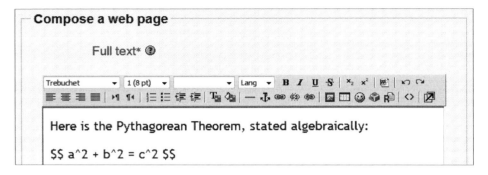

2. To save your changes, click on the **Save and display** button.
3. If all goes well, then the Pythagorean Theorem is displayed:

Here is the Pythagorean Theorem, stated algebraically:

$$a^2 + b^2 = c^2$$

You've probably noticed that I surrounded the math equation with double-dollars ($$). The TeX filter spots the double-dollars and converts the contents into math. The math is actually a TeX image that is usually either in GIF or PNG format depending on how your Moodle is configured, with the alternate text being the TeX used to specify the notation in the image. Try right-clicking on the image to check out the image properties.

Useful TeX notation

Hopefully, you'll find the following table of TeX notation examples useful:

TeX	Resulting output
\pi	π
\sqrt{x}	$\sqrt{x}$
\times	$\times$
\div	$\div$
\infty	∞
\pm	$\pm$
\leq	$\leq$
\geq	$\geq$
a_x	a_x
\equiv	$\equiv$
180^\circ	180°
\neq	$\neq$
\alpha	α
\int	$\int$
\int_{0}^{1}	$\int_0^1$
\theta	θ
\ .\ .\\\ o \\\smile	☺

Remember to enclose your TeX with '**$$**'.

A quick search through a search engine will soon help you locate more comprehensive lists of LaTeX symbols. For example, try `http://www.artofproblemsolving.com/Wiki/index.php/LaTeX:Symbols`.

TeX filter troubleshooting

What if your TeX filter doesn't work and you don't see an image? To test the TeX filter, you'll need to navigate your browser to the TeX filter debug page at `http://www.yourmoodlesite.com/filter/tex/texdebug.php`. Remember to replace `www.yourmoodlesite.com` with the name of your Moodle. Here is a screenshot of the TeX Filter Debugger page:

Please enter an algebraic expression **without** any surrounding $$ into the text box below. (Click here for help.)

> `f(x)=\Bigint_{-\infty}^x~e^{-t^2}dt`

The following tests are available:

1. ⦿ See the cache_filters database entry for this expression (if any).
2. ○ Delete the cache_filters database entry for this expression (if any).
3. ○ Show a graphic image of the algebraic expression rendered with mimetex.
4. ○ Show a graphic image of the algebraic expression rendered with Tex/Ghostscript.
5. ○ Show command execution output from the algebraic expression rendered with Tex/Ghostscript.
6. ○ Check slasharguments setting.

[Do it!]

We explored testing the operation of the Algebra Filter in Chapter 2. The process of testing the TeX filter is much the same. Be sure to test option 3 (**Show a graphic image of the algebraic expression rendered with mimetex.**).

TeX and Ghostscript or ImageMagick will need to be installed on your server unless you are using Mimetex (which is bundled with Moodle in filter/tex).

Let's revisit the **Filters** configuration screen. Remember, you'll need to be signed in as a Moodle administrator. Return to your site's front page and click on **Modules | Filters | TeX Notation**. Here are my TeX settings:

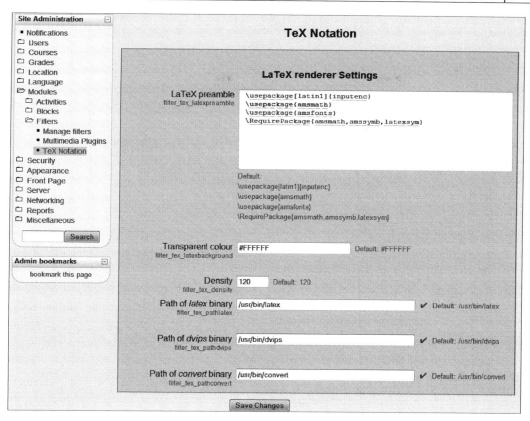

My Moodle is installed on an Ubuntu server, and on that server I have three applications installed: latex, dvips, and convert. You can see from the green tick marks that Moodle has recognized that they are installed. Why do I have those applications installed? The reason is to render better quality mathematical notation. The version of LaTeX you use usually depends on the operating system on your server. Examples include, TeX Live (Unix-type systems, including GNU/Linux), MiKTeX (Windows), or MacTeX (Macintosh). It's worth stressing that if you don't have LaTeX installed on your server, or it isn't working correctly, then the TeX filter will "fall back" to using Mimetex.

There is certainly one scenario in which the TeX filter can go wrong and that's when your Moodle is installed on shared hosting.

The TeX filter on shared hosting

If your Moodle is on shared hosting, then yours is not the only Moodle running on your Moodle server. Shared hosting is usually the cheaper option for hosting a website (which, at the end of the day, is essentially what Moodle is) simply because you are sharing a server with other people. Because you are all sharing the same server, it is quite possible that you could do something that might harm someone else's website and, for that reason, your host will turn off *dangerous* commands. Without going into details, both the Algebra and TeX filters happen to require these commands.

What is the alternative? Both the Algebra and TeX filters generate images of math notation on the server. It is also possible to use external TeX servers to add mathematical notation (in the form of TeX images) directly to your Moodle courses from free sites like these:

- `http://www.sitmo.com/latex/`
- `http://www.codecogs.com/components/equationeditor/equationeditor.php`
- `http://www.mathtran.org/`

But remember: if those sites are closed, you will lose all of your equations.

Also in this chapter, we'll be investigating filters that create TeX images in the browser (see the *Introducing the jsMath filter* section).

TeX filter—further guidance

It's worth noting that different LaTeX distributions may have a different syntax. For example, some custom features of Mimetex are explained at `http://www.forkosh.com/mimetexmanual.html`.

The most complete LaTeX symbol list is found at `http://www.ctan.org/tex-archive/info/symbols/comprehensive/symbols-a4.pdf`. This document lists 4947 symbols and the corresponding LaTeX commands that are needed to produce them. Some of these symbols are guaranteed to be available in every LaTeX system; others require special fonts that may not accompany a given distribution and, therefore, need to be installed separately.

Some good additional examples made for MediaWiki (but can be used with any distribution that has a full AMS package) can be found at `http://meta.wikimedia.org/wiki/Help:Formula`.

Remember to visit the Mathematics Tools forum on Moodle.org (`http://moodle.org/mod/forum/view.php?id=752`.) if you need any help or advice.

Introducing the jsMath filter

Both the Algebra Filter and the TeX filter produce mathematical notation on the server. If your Moodle is hosted by a third party, you might find that the commands needed to create the notation have been disabled by your host (see *The TeX filter on shared hosting*). The alternative is to pass all the details required to construct the notation to the browser and have the browser render it on the client (client-side) rather than on the server (server-side). Having the browser draw the notation requires either built-in (native) support or a plugin. The jsMath filter (`http://moodle.org/mod/data/view.php?d=13&rid=709&filter=1`) attempts just this. This filter, based on the work of Davide Cervone, in fact uses a JavaScript TeX interpreter (hence the name).

Rather than repeating the instructions that are fully available on Moodle.org, check out the installation instructions at `http://cvs.moodle.org/contrib/plugins/filter/jsmath/README.txt?view=markup`.

jsMath can render equations in three ways:

1. By rendering mathematical notation in the browser. This requires the correct font to be installed on the client computer.
2. If step 1 fails, then it attempts to render mathematical notation on the server. This requires the correct fonts to be installed on the server. (Note that there can be a lot of them!)
3. If step 2 fails, then it tries to build equations from Unicode fonts installed on the computer the browser is running on.

What's great about jsMath is that even if your students don't have the correct fonts installed on their computers (if step 1 fails) then, assuming you have the correct fonts installed on the server, the notation is still rendered on the server (step 2).

You can configure jsMath through the jsMath control panel accessible from the bottom-right corner of any web page using jsMath:

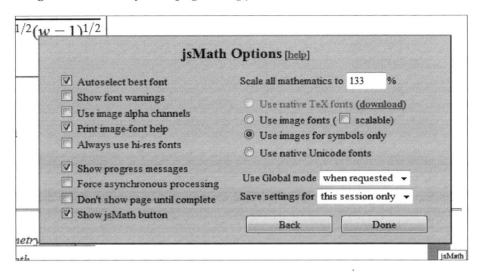

How do you specify math notation using this third type of filter? Don't worry! You simply have to use TeX notation again. Check out the *Useful TeX* notation section in this chapter.

 If the jsMath filter is not working, then make sure your browser's JavaScript support is turned on. Ask your system admin (assuming that's not you) if you're not sure.

DragMath

DragMath is a drag-and-drop equation editor originally developed by Alex Billingsley, under the tutelage of Chris Sangwin, at the University of Birmingham in the UK.

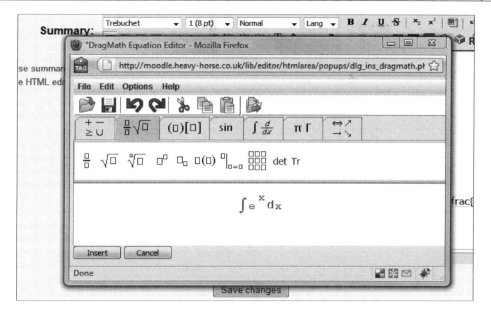

You can see that it looks very similar to the equation editors we first introduced in Chapter 2. However, as you can see, DragMath fully integrates into Moodle. It was originally part of a computer algebra system called STACK, which we introduced in Chapter 6. More details on DragMath can be found in the Moodle docs (`http://docs.moodle.org/en/DragMath_equation_editor`).

Let's start by installing DragMath. You'll need Moodle administrator privileges, and you'll need access to the server Moodle is running on. If you don't have either, then hand this book over to your Moodle administrator now.

Installing DragMath

I'm going to install DragMath on the latest version of Moodle (at the time of writing, this is 1.9.4). If you are using an older version of Moodle, then the installation process will be slightly different; it's all described in the Moodle docs (check out `http://docs.moodle.org/en/DragMath_equation_editor#Installing_DragMath`).

Installing DragMath can require overwriting or modifying core Moodle files. It's a good idea to make a backup of your Moodle installation before you start, just in case something goes wrong.

Rather than simply unzipping the DragMath files directly into my Moodle, I'm going to copy over the DragMath support files from my computer one at a time. This is a good way to get an appreciation of how Moodle's plugin modules integrate into the main system. For the sake of a tool to use, I'm going to be using FileZilla (a free FTP tool from the Mozilla Foundation) running on Windows to perform the file transfers. I'm sure you have your preferences.

Before you start!

Before you start installing DragMath, make sure you put your Moodle into maintenance mode. Log in as an administrator, and select **Server | Maintenance mode** from the **Site Administration** block. This will stop staff and students trying to use Moodle while we are in the middle of updating it.

Follow these steps to install DragMath:

1. Visit `http://download.moodle.org/patches19/dragmath.zip` to download the latest copy of the DragMath Moodle integration files for Moodle 1.9.x versions.

2. Extract the DragMath files to a convenient location on your computer.

3. Open up your FTP client and connect to your Moodle server. Most FTP clients allow you to browse your local computer on one side and browse the remote server on the other:

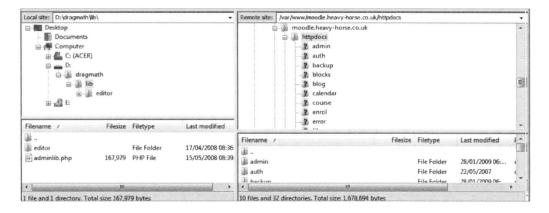

4. Copy the files over to the server from your local machine. The folder names on your local machine will match those on the server. If you have to replace any files, then it is a good idea to rename the files on the server before you copy over any replacements. Note that DragMath distributions can contain a file called `adminlib.php`. Don't replace the `adminlib.php` already in Moodle.

WARNING!
At the time of writing, the DragMath package contains a copy of
`adminlib.php`, which is a core file in Moodle that changes often.
DragMath will still work if you don't copy over `adminlib.php`.

5.   You now have DragMath installed!

Note that the process of installing DragMath is different depending on which version of Moodle you are currently running (see `http://docs.moodle.org/en/DragMath_equation_editor#Installing_DragMath` in the Moodle docs for further details).

Before we let the rabble back in again, the next step is to ensure that DragMath has been installed correctly.

Using DragMath

The first step is to check that the DragMath button has been added to the HTML editor. Then, we'll try using DragMath to generate some math notation. I'm assuming you're still logged into Moodle as an administrator.

You'll need to get the TeX filter turned on and functioning properly before DragMath will work correctly. For those readers dipping in at this point, we cover configuring the TeX filter at the beginning of this chapter.

Verifying your DragMath installation

We need to open up a configuration page that contains the HTML editor. Return to your site's front page (don't worry if it is blank: remember, you are in maintenance mode), and click on your username. Mine's at the top-right of the page:

1. Click on the **Edit profile** tab, and scroll down the page until you reach the **Description** edit area. Do you see the new DragMath button?

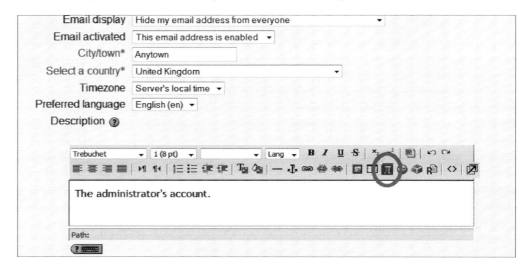

2. Click on the DragMath button. The DragMath window will appear with a dialog giving a security warning:

3. Make sure the option **Always trust content from this publisher** is selected, and click on the **Run** button.

4. DragMath is displayed:

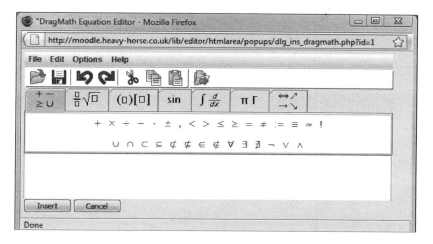

5. Now, let's create a simple fraction using DragMath's drag-and-drop editor. Select the fraction/root tab and click on the fraction icon:

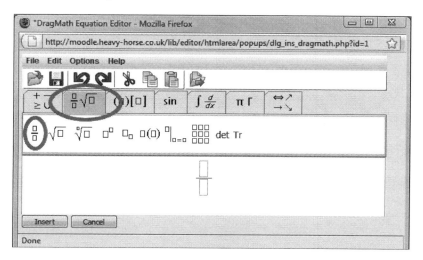

6. Click on the numerator and type it in. Do the same with the denominator. Your fraction is now ready to insert into the editor. Click on the **Insert** button. DragMath will create the required TeX notation and insert it into the HTML editor:

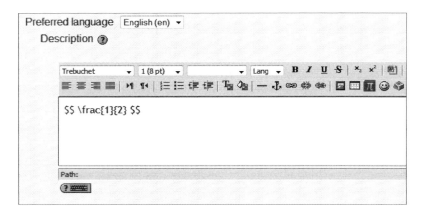

7. Remember: Moodle is still in maintenance mode, and we are testing DragMath using our profile description. You will need to update your profile to see if the fraction is displayed correctly:

8. DragMath is now ready to use! When you are happy that everything is working as it should be, remember to disable maintenance mode.

We've just seen that installing DragMath has added a new button to the HTML editor and that clicking on the button correctly opens DragMath. We've also experimented with creating a simple fraction. We found that the benefit of installing DragMath is that it creates TeX notation automatically, without us having to learn TeX.

Supporting multiple Moodles: Hiding the DragMath button

Sometimes it is required that we hide buttons on the HTML editor. Perhaps your Moodle is one of many being maintained centrally which, for the sake of convenience and to make support much easier, all have the same modules and plugins installed. Some of the schools in your domain may have no need for the DragMath button and don't want it included in their HTML editors. You can configure which buttons are available and which are hidden from the **Site Administration** block, under **Appearance | HTML editor**. To include it, we need to modify `adminlib.php`. (That's why there's a copy of `adminlib.php` included in the DragMath package; but again, it's best to modify the version of `adminlib.php` on your server, rather than using the one bundled with DragMath.) Let's do that now!

As an alternative to FileZilla, I'm going to be using `putty.exe` running on Windows to access my server. Then, I'll use the text editor `nano` to edit `adminlib.php`:

1. Log on to your server, and open `adminlib.php` ready for editing.

2. Search within `adminlib.php` for the line **'insertsmile' => 'em.icon.smile.gif'**:

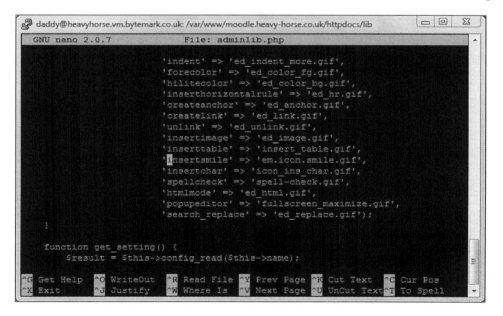

3. Immediately after, add in the line **'insertdragmath' => 'em.icon.dragmath. gif'** as shown:

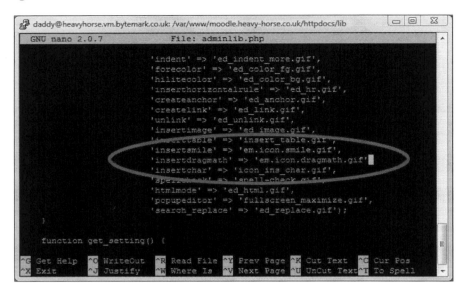

4. In your browser, navigate back to the HTML editor configuration page. Refresh it if you are already there. You will now be able to hide the DragMath button:

5. Select the DragMath option to hide the button. That's it! We're done.

Hiding the DragMath button—recap

We've just modified `adminlib.php` so that we can allow admins to hide the DragMath button if they want to. If you are maintaining a number of Moodles and happen to be installing the same modules and plugins in all of them, then we can't assume that all of those schools will want the DragMath button to be available in their HTML editors.

When editing `adminlib.php` and inserting the line
`'insertdragmath' => 'em.icon.dragmath.gif',`
don't forget the comma on the end!

Using DragMath with different filters

By default, DragMath will create TeX notation, which the TeX filter can then convert into math notation. But DragMath doesn't just create TeX. Open DragMath and choose **Options | Set export format** from DragMath's main menu. In the options dialog, you can now choose the format of notation DragMath will automatically generate:

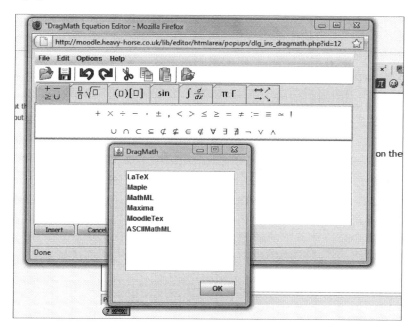

Why the different options? Because DragMath wasn't designed just for Moodle. To select the output format, simply click on the format you require and click **OK**. Check out the **ASCIIMathML** option. We'll be investigating ASCIIMathML later on in this chapter.

What if you're having trouble getting DragMath to work? Let's spend the final section on DragMath investigating what might possibly go wrong.

When DragMath is Installed and Tested

Remember to disable **Maintenance mode**. Return to the **Site Administration** block, select **Server | Maintenance mode**, and click on the **disable** button.

DragMath troubleshooting

You don't see the DragMath button in your HTML editor toolbar. Repeat the steps outlined in the *Installing DragMath* section to ensure there isn't a step you might have accidentally missed.

- The DragMath window is open but stays empty. Make sure the Java Runtime Environment (JRE) version 1.5 or higher is installed on your computer. Java can be downloaded from `http://java.com/en/download/index.jsp`.

- Make sure file permissions are set correctly on the server. Ensure that the files you copied over have **Read**, **Write**, and **Execute** permissions set to allow for the **Owner** and the **Group** but that the **Public** permissions are just set to **Read**. In FileZilla, go back to Moodle's `lib` directory, right-click on the `lib` directory, and select **File Attributes** from the menu. In the **Change file attributes** dialog, ensure the **Recurse into subdirectories** option is ticked and click **OK**. Now all files and folders will have the correct permissions:

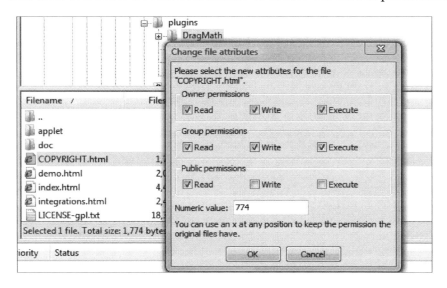

- Also ensure that the directory permissions are also set correctly (a common mistake). You may need to give the DragMath directory **Public Execute** permissions in order for the DragMath applet to run:

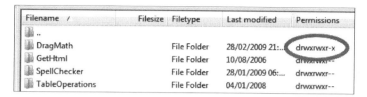

- Make sure local permissions are set correctly. Especially in a school or college environment, a good deal of the permissions required to run Java might well be denied. Visit `java.com` for more information on required permissions. If your college network is managed by a third party, then it is best to discuss your requirements with them so that they can reset client permissions accordingly.

- `adminlib.php` is out of date. As previously mentioned, `adminlib.php` is a file that is almost constantly being developed. As such, you may find that if you are experiencing strange behavior with your Moodle after having just installed DragMath, then it is worth restoring the original copy of `adminlib.php`. For more information on this issue, check out `http://docs.moodle.org/en/DragMath_equation_editor` in the Moodle docs.

Resizing the HTML editor toolbar

Now that a new button has been added to the HTML editor toolbar, you may find that in some situations the rightmost button on the second row (the Enlarge Editor button) is now protruding out of the side of the editor:

Depending on factors such as the browser you are using or the zoom level, it's not a problem that affects all users. It also depends on the page on which the editor is included. Resizing the toolbar and HTML area to accommodate (more neatly) the new DragMath button takes a little tweaking of the Moodle code. Take a look in the Moodle forums (`http://moodle.org/mod/forum/discuss.php?d=84724`) for more information on this issue.

Now that we've got DragMath installed and ready to use, let's look at installing ASCIIMathML, which is the topic of the next section.

ASCIIMathML

Recall that to include a simple fraction in a Moodle course using the TeX filter, I was required to type in `$$\frac{1}{2}$$`. The Algebra Filter simplifies things a little, using a more natural notation: `@@1/2@@`. However, while great for simple notation, we soon reach the limit of the capabilities of the Algebra Filter. There is yet another problem with both filters: the math notation they produce is rendered in an image, and it's actually a little picture of the math that's included in our courses. That means if you've a visually impaired student in your course who uses a screenreader for access then, unless he/she knows LaTeX, your math is going to be almost totally inaccessible. That's where MathML comes in. MathML is a standard from the W3C to enable fully accessible mathematical notation to be included in web pages (full details are found at `http://www.w3.org/Math/`). As far as how the notation looks on the screen is concerned, you probably wouldn't notice the difference between math written to an image and math rendered directly using MathML. The difference is that notation rendered via MathML is fully accessible to all modern screenreaders. However, MathML is incredibly difficult to create without specialist tools. That's where the ASCIIMathML filter comes in. With ASCIIMathML installed, we'll be able to create fully accessible math using a natural notation. Let's get on and install that ASCIIMathML filter.

Installing ASCIIMathML

Installing ASCIIMathML can be a little involved, but it is well worth the effort as we shall see in this and the next chapter (when we will be including graphs in our courses):

 Internet Explorer doesn't include native support for MathML, so I'm going to be installing and testing ASCIIMathML using Firefox. We'll be configuring IE to support MathML later in this section.

1. Download the latest version of ASCIIMathML from SourceForge (`http://sourceforge.net/project/showfiles.php?group_id=106148`).

2. Navigate to your Moodle installation. Create a new folder under **filter** called **asciimath**:

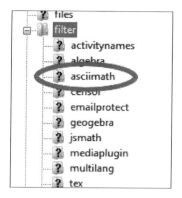

3. Copy the ASCIIMathML files you've just downloaded from SourceForge into the new folder:

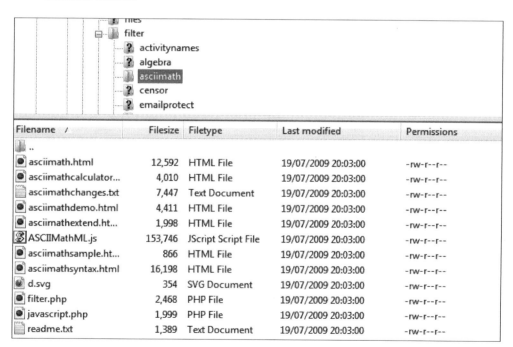

Filename /	Filesize	Filetype	Last modified	Permissions
..				
asciimath.html	12,592	HTML File	19/07/2009 20:03:00	-rw-r--r--
asciimathcalculator...	4,010	HTML File	19/07/2009 20:03:00	-rw-r--r--
asciimathchanges.txt	7,447	Text Document	19/07/2009 20:03:00	-rw-r--r--
asciimathdemo.html	4,411	HTML File	19/07/2009 20:03:00	-rw-r--r--
asciimathextend.ht...	1,998	HTML File	19/07/2009 20:03:00	-rw-r--r--
ASCIIMathML.js	153,746	JScript Script File	19/07/2009 20:03:00	-rw-r--r--
asciimathsample.ht...	866	HTML File	19/07/2009 20:03:00	-rw-r--r--
asciimathsyntax.html	16,198	HTML File	19/07/2009 20:03:00	-rw-r--r--
d.svg	354	SVG Document	19/07/2009 20:03:00	-rw-r--r--
filter.php	2,468	PHP File	19/07/2009 20:03:00	-rw-r--r--
javascript.php	1,999	PHP File	19/07/2009 20:03:00	-rw-r--r--
readme.txt	1,389	Text Document	19/07/2009 20:03:00	-rw-r--r--

4. ASCIIMathML has now been installed as a new filter. Navigate to your Moodle site's front page and, from the **Site Administration** block, select **Modules | Filters | Manage filters**. **Asciimathml** will now be listed:

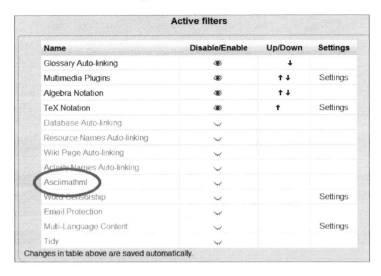

5. Don't worry about turning on the **Asciimathml** filter. For now, you just need to disable the TeX and Algebra filters.

6. Let's test out the filter. The best way of doing this is to create a Moodle web page resource (I'm going to use a test course I have just for this purpose):

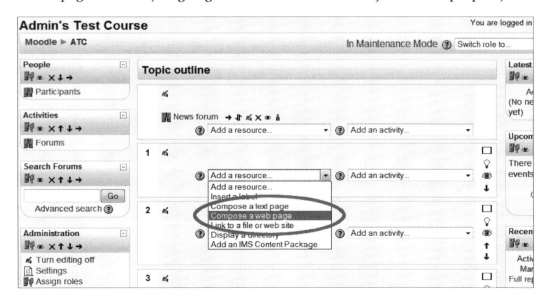

7. In the HTML editor, type in `` `1/2` ``. Note the use of back-quotes `` ` `` rather than apostrophes ':

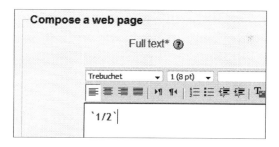

8. Click on the **Save and display** button. The fraction $\frac{1}{2}$ is now displayed:

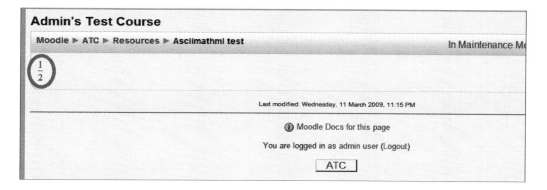

9. That means ASCIIMathML is now installed and working in our Moodle!

Why didn't we need to enable the ASCIIMathML filter?

Because of the way the ASCIIMathML filter has been written, Moodle will use asciimathml no matter if we have enabled the filter or not. So, how do you control the filter? The best way is to enable it via a Moodle theme. To do that, we first need to move the asciimath directory we created on the server out of the filter directory. I'm going to move mine to the Moodle root directory:

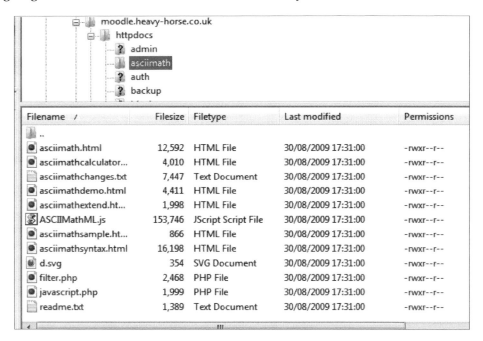

Enabling ASCIIMathML in your Moodle theme

Now that we've moved the ASCIIMathML filter out of Moodle's filter directory, we need to enable the filter by inserting a fragment of HTML at the top of every Moodle page. The practical way to do this is to insert it automatically using the current Moodle theme. This may not sound obvious at first, but let's run through the process now:

1. You will need to log on to the server running Moodle and navigate to the Moodle theme directory. I'm using FileZilla running on a Windows computer to do this. The theme I'm currently employing is standardwhite (You can verify your theme from the **Site Administration** block. Click on **Appearance | Themes | Theme Selector**.):

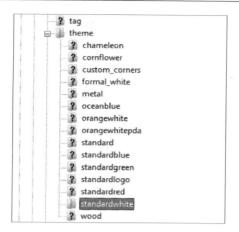

2. Create a new file on your computer. (if you are using Windows, you can use Notepad or WordPad to do this). Call the new file `meta.php`.

3. Type the following into the `meta.php` file:

```
<script type="text/javascript" src="<?php echo $CFG->httpswwwroot
?>/asciimath/ASCIIMathML.js"></script>.
```

4. Save `meta.php` and upload it to your theme directory on the server:

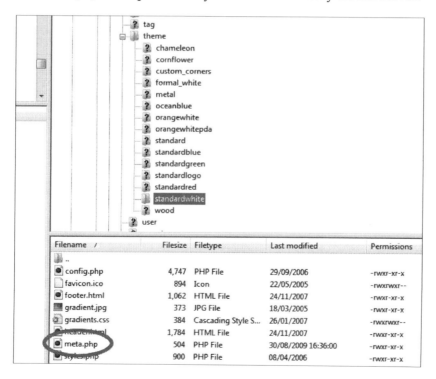

5. We now need to configure Moodle to look for the `meta.php` file. I'm going to navigate FileZilla to the directory Moodle is installed in and open the `config.php` file for editing:

sso	File Folder	29/03/2007		drwxr-xr-x
stack-dev	File Folder	16/07/2009 23:47:00		drwxr-xr-x
tag	File Folder	25/09/2008		drwxr-xr-x
theme	File Folder	28/01/2009		drwxr-xr-x
user	File Folder	28/01/2009		drwxr-xr-x
userpix	File Folder	11/07/2008		drwxr-xr-x
config-dist.php	17,236	PHP File	01/07/2008	-rwxr-xr-x
config.php	762	PHP File	20/04/2009 01:12:00	-rwxr-xr-x
file.php	7,722	PHP File	11/07/2008	-rwxr-xr-x
help.php	7,549	PHP File	18/06/2008	-rwxr-xr-x
index.php	11,870	PHP File	20/09/2008	-rwxr-xr-x
install.php	49,693	PHP File	20/11/2008	-rwxr-xr-x
manifest.txt	94,446	Text Document	11/07/2008	-rwxrwxr--
README.txt	947	Text Document	15/11/2007	-rwxrwxr--

6. Open the `config.php` file for editing. Include the line `$THEME->metainclude = TRUE;` :

```
$CFG->dbpersist   =  false;
$CFG->prefix      = 'mdl_';

$CFG->wwwroot     = 'http://moodle.heavy-horse.co.uk';
$CFG->dirroot     = '/var/www/moodle.heavy-horse.co.uk/httpdocs';
$CFG->dataroot    = '/var/www/moodle.heavy-horse.co.uk/moodledata'
$CFG->admin       = 'admin';

$CFG->directorypermissions = 00777;  // try 02777 on a server in
Mode

$THEME->metainclude = TRUE;

require_once("$CFG->dirroot/lib/setup.php");
// MAKE SURE WHEN YOU EDIT THIS FILE THAT THERE ARE NO SPACES, B
LINES,
// RETURNS, OR ANYTHING ELSE AFTER THE TWO CHARACTERS ON THE NEX
LINE.
?>
```

7. I'm now going to return to Moodle and to my test course. Delete the previous Moodle web page, and now add in a new ASCIIMathML test page. Try adding in a simple fraction such as \`1/2\`. Your math notation will be displayed as normal. The HTML code from `meta.php` will be inserted automatically at the top of the page (you can view the source to ensure this is the case).

Including support for MathML in Internet Explorer

To achieve support for MathML, you will need to install MathPlayer, a special add-on available from Design Science Inc. at `http://www.dessci.com/en/products/mathplayer/download.htm`. Simply follow the instructions to install the add-on, and test the installation by navigating IE to the Moodle web page we created earlier in this section.

Right-click on the fraction, and you'll notice that MathPlayer includes some powerful accessibility options, including a zoom function (MathZoom) and the option to read the fraction out loud using Window's built-in text-to-speech facilities (Speak Expression):

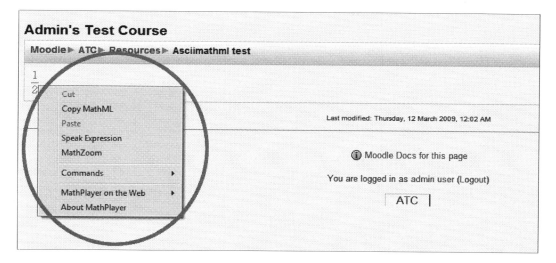

Browser requirements

Aside from the browser having to support MathML, one of the important differences between the TeX and Algebra filters is that they render the math notation on the server. ASCIIMathML renders the notation in the browser (on the client computer). That means the correct fonts need to be installed on the client. If needed, these can be downloaded from Mozilla.org (`http://www.mozilla.org/projects/mathml/fonts/`).

ASCIIMathML with fallback

Clearly, we can't expect every computer/browser to have support for MathML installed. To that end, a version of ASCIIMathML that provides a fallback mechanism has been produced. This version is called `ASCIIMathML2wMnGFallback.js` and is available to download from `http://groups.google.com/group/asciimath`. The file specifies a variable giving the location of a Mimetex executable to fall back to:

You will probably want to modify the script to point to a copy of Mimetex on your server (unless you are using some external service). It's worth mentioning that this script can be modified further to support any TeX renderer.

Simply back up the original copy of ASCIIMathML.js, and replace it with `ASCIIMathML2wMnGFallback.js`.

ASCIIMathML further options

Remember how we mentioned that ASCIIMathML requires a special fragment of HTML code from `meta.php`? You can complement that with more code that configures how the math is displayed:

```
<script type="text/javascript">
var mathcolor = "black";
var mathfontfamily = "STIXGeneral,Arial Unicode MS,"Lucida Sans
Unicode","Lucida Grande",Garuda,sans-serif";
</script>
```

Experiment with the `mathcolor` and `mathfontfamily` variables (especially with fonts that have serifs and those that don't) to explore the various ways in which math can be displayed. You might want to specify different fonts to support different operating systems. If you don't specify a `mathfontfamily` variable, then the browser's default font is used.

Now that we have ASCIIMathML enabled via the Moodle theme, you could consider having a special Moodle theme just for those courses that require ASCIIMathML.

Summary

In this chapter, we learned how to create more complex mathematical notation and make our notation far more accessible. We also learned how to speed up the process of including math notation in our courses by installing DragMath—a drag-and-drop equation editor that installs directly into Moodle's HTML editor. Up to now, the notation we have inserted into our courses has primarily been in the form of mathematical notation rendered in an image. This image isn't directly accessible to any user who is blind or visually impaired, unless he/she is familiar with TeX. One solution is to generate math using MathML. This isn't natively supported by all browsers, so we investigated how this support could be added into Internet Explorer.

Specifically, we covered these topics:

* Installing and using the TeX filter for more advanced mathematical notation
* How jsMath overcomes problems with web hosting providers who don't provide all the commands we need to make the TeX filter operate correctly
* Installing and using the DragMath equation editor to generate math notation directly in Moodle
* How to install and use ASCIIMathML to produce accessible mathematics notation

So far, we have been concentrating on math notation. ASCIIMathML doesn't just support notation. It also includes a very powerful graphing tool called ASCIIsvg. In the next chapter, we'll be continuing the work begun here with ASCIIMathML by investigating how to include graphs in our Moodle courses.

8

Graphs and Charts

In the previous chapter we concentrated on mathematical notation and various ways we can generate it and include it in our courses. We ended the previous chapter investigating ASCIIMathML, a Moodle filter that allows us to incorporate accessible mathematics using a natural form of notation (no need to learn TeX). ASCIIMathML includes a powerful component that allows us to easily incorporate graphs of functions. This leads on to thinking about how to include graphs and charts into our courses. One way of doing so is to simply draw the graph or chart and scan it in. However, this method isn't very flexible and also not very accessible. In this chapter, we will investigate the tools that we can use to create graphs and charts and learn how to incorporate them into our courses.

In this chapter, we shall cover these topics:

- Incorporating graphs into our courses using ASCIIsvg
- Creating charts in Microsoft Office and OpenOffice.org and the best ways to include these in our courses
- Investigate Google Charts and the Chart API

We'll begin by building on our work with ASCIIMathML and by learning how we can use ASCIIMathML and ASCIIsvg to include graphs of functions in our courses.

ASCIIMathML and ASCIIsvg

The ASCIIMathML plugin also contains ASCIIsvg, a powerful tool for creating graphs of functions. What's great about ASCIIsvg is that we can use simple commands to create quite complex graphs and diagrams.

Let's start by including a graph of a simple function in our course using ASCIIsvg, in this case a graph of $y=x^2$. Note that for this exercise I'm going to use Firefox, which includes built-in support for SVG graphics. Don't worry! We'll look at how other browsers support SVG in a later section.

Including graphs using ASCIIsvg

I'm going to include my graph on a Moodle web page. I've chosen a topic, clicked on the **Add a resource** drop-down list, and selected **Compose a web page**:

1. We can specify the function we want to plot directly into the HTML editor. I'm going to plot this graph in the simplest way possible by using a single command: plot(x^2). Don't forget to enclose the ASCIIsvg commands in single quotes:

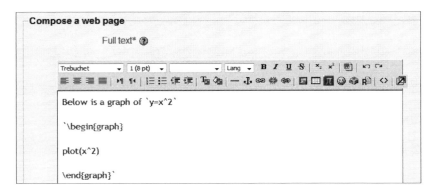

2. Scroll down and click on the **Save and display** button. The graph of **y=x²** is displayed:

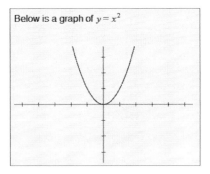

Note that the commands we use to plot a graph need to be enclosed in \begin{graph} and \end{graph}. Remember to enclose all ASCIIsvg commands (including \begin{graph} and \end{graph}) in single quotes.

Try moving the cursor over the graph. Do you see the coordinates displayed? If you have to describe a graph to a class, then use ASCIIsvg in Moodle and an interactive white board. It makes a great solution!

Basic ASCIIsvg commands

The ASCIIsvg command that you may find yourself using the most is plot(). This command not only plots f(x), but it also plots parametric equations, f(t) and g(t). plot() supports all of the following functions: +, -, *, /, ^, pi, e, sqrt(), ln(), abs(), sign(), floor(), ceil(), n!, C(n,k), ran(a,b,n), sin(), cos(), tan(), sin^-1(), cos^-1(), tan^-1(), sinh(), cosh(), tanh(), sinh^-1(), cosh^-1(), tanh^-1(), sech(), csch(), coth(), sech^-1(), csch^-1(), coth^-1(). plot() also supports all valid JavaScript math constants or functions.

 The symbol ^ means to the power of. But sin^-1() will determine the arc sine for a given ratio. Note that all the trigonometric functions expect and provide angles in radians.

In the following table, you'll find the basic commands supported by ASCIIsvg and a brief explanation of their meaning along with examples.

Command	Meaning	Comments
initPicture(xmin,xmax, ymin,ymax)	Specifies the axis ranges. ymin and ymax are optional. If ymin is omitted, then the origin will be positioned in the middle of the graph. If ymax is omitted, then ymax = xmax.	initPicture(-2,2,-2,2)

axes()	Draws the coordinate axes on a graph.	`\begin{graph}`
		`initPicture(-2,2,-2,2)`
		`axes()`
		`\end{graph}`

Command	Meaning	Comments
`line([x1,y1],[x2,y2])`	Draws a line from x1,y1 to x2,y2.	 ``` `\begin{graph} initPicture(-2,2,-2,2) axes() line([-1,-1],[1,1]) \end{graph}` ```
`marker="symbol"`	Specifies a symbol to be drawn at one or the other end of the line.	A symbol can take the following values: dot, arrow, arrowdot, or none. ``` `\begin{graph} initPicture(-2,2,-2,2) axes() marker="arrowdot" line([-1,-1],[1,1]) \end{graph}` ```
`stroke="color"`	Specifies the pen color.	Color can be both the name of a color, say red, or it's RGB value. An RGB value is a special number that gives the relative proportions of red, green, and blue for a particular color. See `http://en.wikipedia.org/wiki/RGB_color_model#Numeric_representations` for more information.

Command	Meaning	Comments
`circle([x,y],r)`	Draws a circle with origin (x,y) and radius r.	 ``` `\begin{graph} initPicture(-2,2,-2,2) axes() circle([0,0],1) \end{graph}` ```
`strokewidth="value"`	Specifies the width in pixels of the line, curve, and so on.	 ``` `\begin{graph} initPicture(-2,2,-2,2) axes() strokewidth="4" line([-1,-1],[1,1]) \end{graph}` ```
`text([x,y],"label" {,position})`	Prints label at coordinates (x,y) at the specified position.	Position can take the following values: above, below, left, right, aboveleft, aboveright, belowleft, or belowright. ``` `\begin{graph} initPicture(-10,10,-10,10) grid() plot(x^2-4) text([0,-4],"Vertex",belowright) \end{graph}` ```

More information on ASCIIsvg commands can be found at
`http://www1.chapman.edu/~jipsen/svg/asciisvgcommands.html`.

More ASCIIsvg examples

Using ASCIIsvg opens up further opportunities to explore mathematics:

1. Explore solving simultaneous equations graphically: For example, find the coordinates of the points of intersection of the line and the circle:

$$y = 5 - \frac{1}{3}x$$

$$x^2 + y^2 = 25$$

2. However, it is easy with ASCIIsvg. Simply hover the mouse pointer over the points where the circle and the line meet:

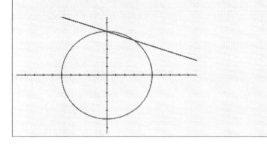

Calculate the coordinates of the points of intersection of the line and the circle...

$$y = 5 - \frac{1}{3}x$$
$$x^2 + y^2 = 25$$

You can hover your mouse pointer over the points of intersection on the graph below to confirm your results:

3. Here is how I composed this page:

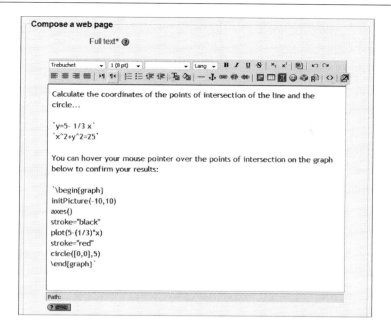

Note that I used two separate commands to plot a line and the circle. For the line, I used **plot(5-(1/3)*x)**. To plot the red circle, I used the command **circle([0,0],5)**, a circle with its origin where the coordinate axes cross and a radius of 5.

4. Recognizing graphs: Use Moodle quizzes to test your students and to see if they can match the graph with its equation:

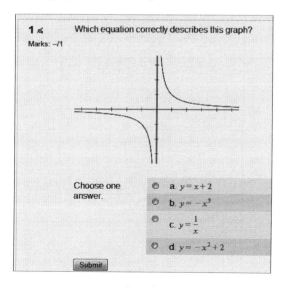

5. Here is the **Question text**:

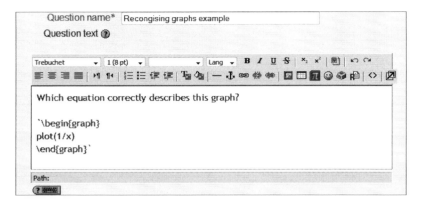

6. Enclosing the answers in back ticks means the ASCIIMathML filter will convert the answer into mathematical notation:

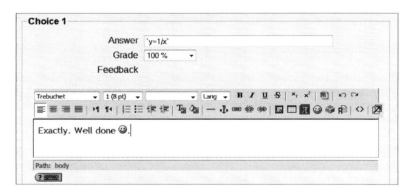

7. Transforming graphs: Demonstrate what happens to a graph when it is transformed:

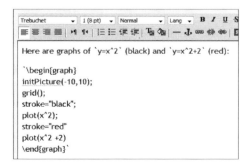

8. This is the result:

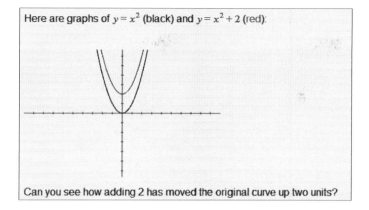

Here are graphs of $y = x^2$ (black) and $y = x^2 + 2$ (red):

Can you see how adding 2 has moved the original curve up two units?

9. Exploring parametric equations: Until now, I've been using the `plot()` command to plot the relationship between two variables. But the plot command supports parametric equations, too. That means producing graphs of parametric equations is easy with ASCIIsvg. Here is a screenshot of the edited page on parametric equations:

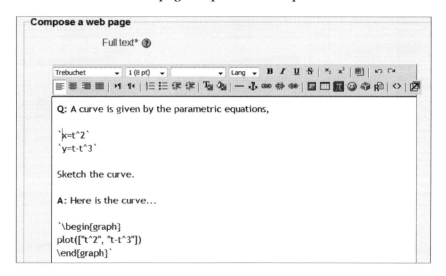

10. It is displayed as this:

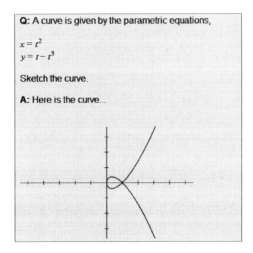

> **Q:** A curve is given by the parametric equations,
>
> $x = t^2$
> $y = t - t^3$
>
> Sketch the curve.
>
> **A:** Here is the curve...

ASCIIsvg browser support

The reason why I was careful to stress that I was going to be using Firefox to test ASCIIsvg (and the reason why all of the previous examples of ASCIIsvg use screenshots of Firefox) is that Firefox ships with built-in support for SVG graphics. However, the most popular browser (at time of writing), Internet Explorer, doesn't. Try opening a chart in Internet Explorer. Here's what you'll probably see:

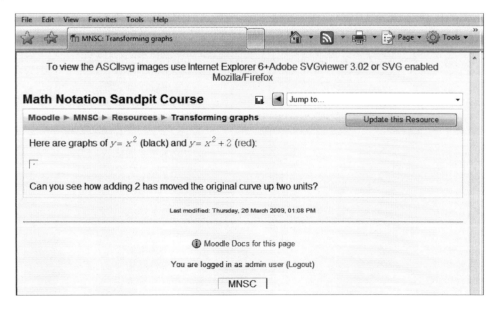

I've already got MathPlayer installed so the equations display correctly. The graph, however, isn't displayed; Internet Explorer doesn't support SVG images, so I need to install a special add-on for that, too. The add-on I need is Adobe's SVG viewer. A link to the viewer home page is inserted at the top of the page. To download and install SVG viewer, you will need to visit `http://www.adobe.com/svg/viewer/install/`.

Once the viewer is installed, your graphs will be displayed correctly.

If you want to use ASCIIsvg to display graphs, then it is worth considering that students using computers outside your school or college may be using a browser that doesn't have SVG support installed.

Support for SVG is included in Firefox, Opera, Amaya, Konqueror, and Safari. For more information on browser support, visit `http://en.wikipedia.org/wiki/Scalable_Vector_Graphics#Support_for_SVG_in_web_browsers`.

Creating charts in Microsoft Excel and OpenOffice.org Calc

A simple way of creating charts to include in our courses is to use a spreadsheet application and then copy them over to Moodle. In this section, we will be investigating the two most popular spreadsheet applications: Microsoft Excel and OpenOffice.org. Let's start with Microsoft Excel.

Creating charts with Microsoft Excel

In this example, I'm going to use Microsoft Office Excel 2003. The process we will be working through is the same for later versions of Excel. Note that it will also work with earlier versions, but you might have to hunt for the functions.

Here is a data handling question I am going to set for my students:

A workshop manager carried out a survey to find out how long people spent drinking refreshments during their morning break. Below is his data:

Time (t seconds)	Number
$0 < t \leq 30$	4
$30 < t \leq 60$	10
$60 < t \leq 90$	15
$90 < t \leq 120$	17
$120 < t \leq 150$	3

a) Draw a cumulative frequency curve for this data.

b) Find the median time spent drinking refreshments.

c) Find the interquartile range.

As part of an explanation of how to answer this question, I want to include the cumulative frequency curve in my course. Let's start by copying the question data into Excel.

Creating a chart in Microsoft Excel

I've introduced two columns into the table; these will allow me to plot a chart of Time versus Cumulative Frequency:

1. Select the x and y columns from the table:

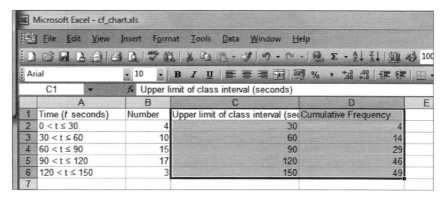

2. From the main menu, choose **Insert | Chart** (Excel 2007 users need to select from the ribbon's **Charts** section). The **Chart Wizard** is displayed. Choose **XY (Scatter)** and select "Scatter" as the chart sub-type (Excel 2007 users can select that chart type directly from the ribbon):

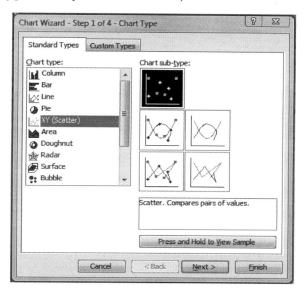

3. Press the **Next** (or **OK**) button to continue. Ensure that Excel knows the data series it is plotting is in columns. For our cumulative frequency example, you'll be able to see immediately if the plot isn't an ogive – a smooth S-shape:

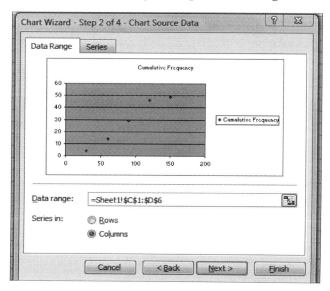

4. Now, click on the **Next** button. Use the **Chart Options** page to label your axes and set the x and y ranges, if necessary:

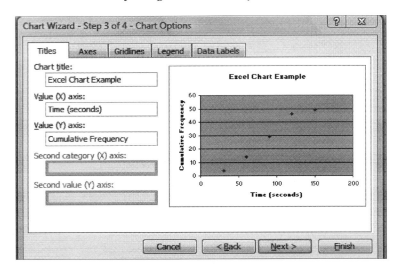

5. Click on the **Next** button. In the final step, let's insert the chart as a new sheet:

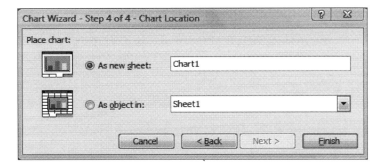

6. Click on the **Finish** button. The new chart is now inserted into the workbook. Next, we need to draw a trendline through these points. Select **Chart | Add Trendline**. The **Add Trendline** dialog is displayed. I'm going to choose a third-order polynomial trendline (as an approximate best fit):

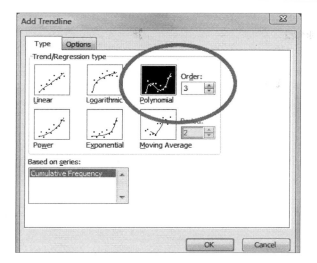

7. The trendline is now drawn on the graph:

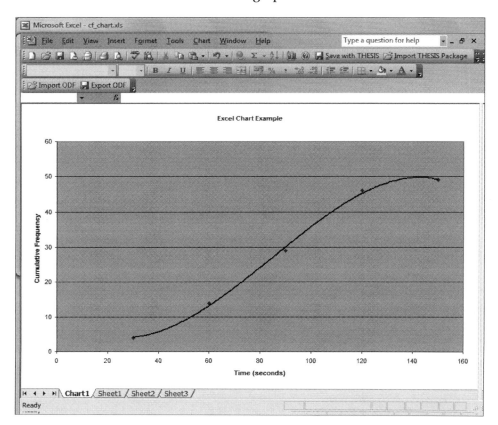

8. Now, we need to insert the chart into Moodle. One option would be to save the Excel workbook, upload this to our Moodle course, and make it available to our students on the course's front page. Note that we are assuming our students have access to Excel on the computer they are using:

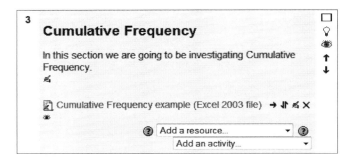

9. If you don't want to rely on your students having Excel installed, then save the chart as a web page. Choose **File | Save As**, and select **Web Page** from the **Save as type** drop-down menu:

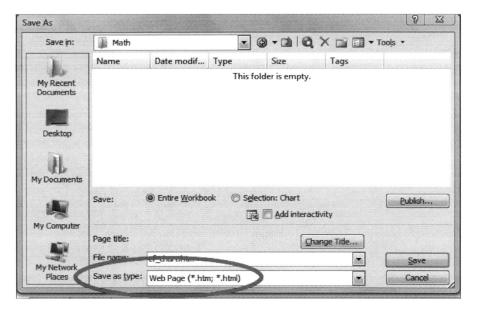

10. Navigate your file browser to the folder in which you've just saved your chart. In there, you'll find a folder with the same name as your HTM document suffixed with `_files`. In that folder you'll find a GIF image of your chart. You can include this image directly into your Moodle course using the HTML editor's **Insert Image** button. I've included it in a Moodle web page:

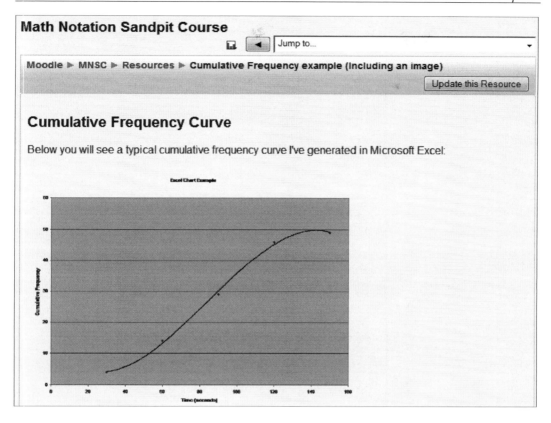

Including an Excel chart in a Moodle course—recap

We've just learned how to create a chart in Microsoft Excel and investigated two ways of including that chart in a Moodle course: upload the Excel workbook as is or save the chart as an image. Saving the chart as an image means we don't have to rely on our students having Microsoft Excel installed on their computers.

If you are a Microsoft Excel 2007 user, then your students might have trouble opening an .xlsx file. There is a special file converter that can be installed in older versions of Excel. You can also save the workbook as a previous Excel file version.

For more information, visit http://office.microsoft.com/en-us/help/HA100775611033.aspx.

Creating charts with OpenOffice.org Calc

OpenOffice.org Calc and Microsoft Excel are very similar applications – except that OpenOffice.org Calc is free! In the following example, I need to create a horizontal bar chart showing the favorite colors in my class. Here is the data:

Color	Frequency
Brown	3
Yellow	4
Green	9
Red	13
Blue	8

Creating a bar graph in OpenOffice.org Calc

Let's create a bar graph in Calc and include that in our Moodle course:

1. I've entered the data for the bar chart in a new spreadsheet:

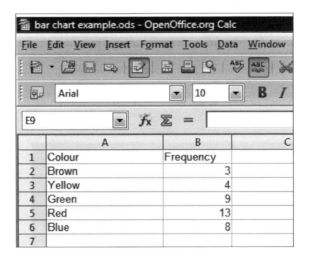

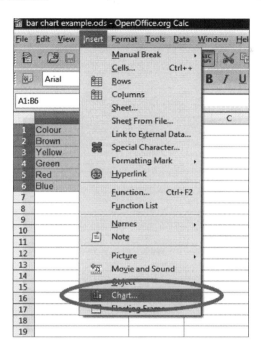

2. Select the **Color** and **Frequency** columns, and then choose **Insert | Chart** from the main menu:

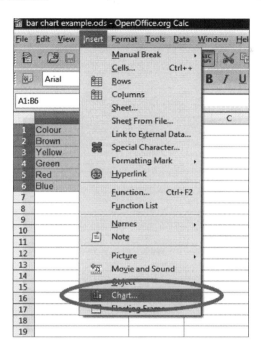

3. The **Chart Wizard** is displayed. Select the horizontal bar chart type. We have already chosen the **Data Range** and **Data Series**. Click on **Chart Elements**:

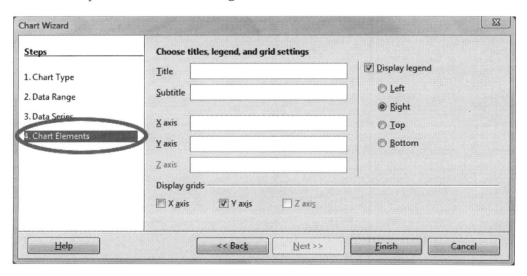

4. Specify a title for your chart. You can also label the axes. I'm also going to hide the chart legend:

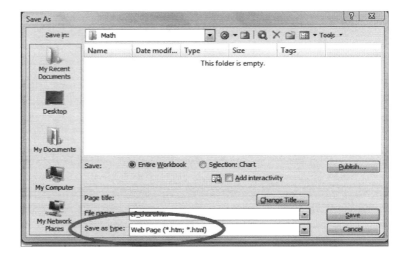

5. Click on the **Finish** button. A new horizontal bar chart has now been added to our spreadsheet. All we need to do now is insert it into our course. Choose **Select File | Save As** from the main menu, and save the spreadsheet as an **HTML Document**:

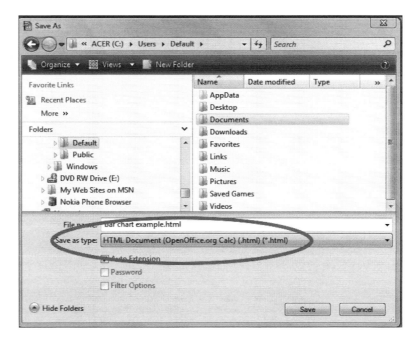

6. Take a look inside the folder to which you just saved the spreadsheet. Calc will have created a copy of the chart as a JPG image:

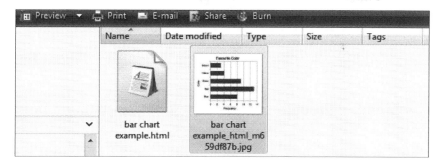

7. Return to your Moodle course. Turn on editing, choose a topic, and then choose **compose a web page**. Include the chart by inserting an image:

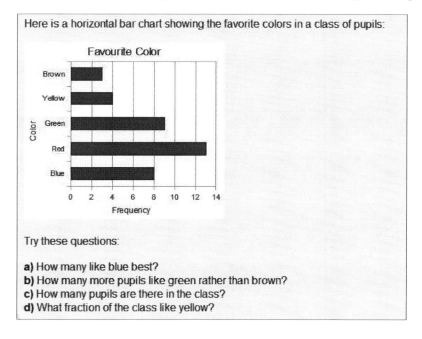

Here is a horizontal bar chart showing the favorite colors in a class of pupils:

Try these questions:

a) How many like blue best?
b) How many more pupils like green rather than brown?
c) How many pupils are there in the class?
d) What fraction of the class like yellow?

8. That's it! We're done.

Creating graphs and charts in Calc is much the same as in Microsoft Excel; they are very similar applications.

Google Docs

Google Docs is a free online office productivity suite that includes Google Spreadsheets. You will need a Google account to sign into Google Docs. To access Google Docs, you will need to visit `http://docs.google.com`. Once you are logged in to Google Docs, select **Create new | Spreadsheet** from the main menu. A new window is opened containing a new, unsaved spreadsheet:

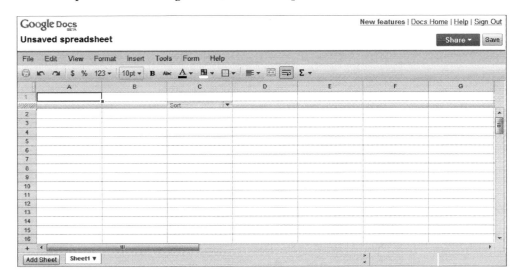

I surveyed my class to see what type of music they like. I've entered this data into the spreadsheet:

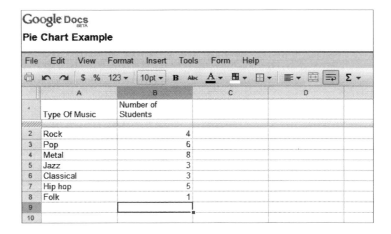

In the next section, we'll create a pie chart and include it in our Moodle course.

Creating a pie chart in Google Spreadsheets

Follow these steps to create a pie chart in Google spreadsheets:

1. Select the two columns of data. Choose **Insert | Chart** from the main menu:

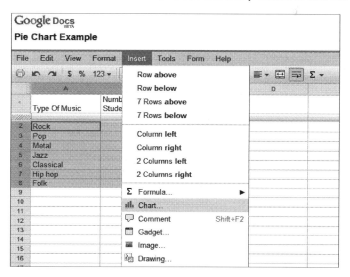

2. In the **Create chart** dialog, select **Pie**. You can also specify a pie chart with a 3D effect:

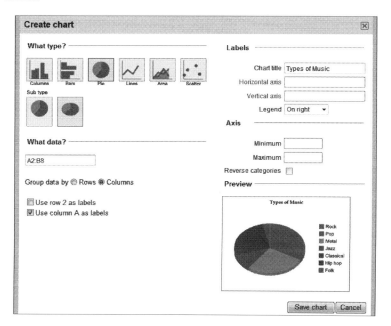

3. Click on the **Save chart** button. Click on a sector, and the details of that sector (number of students and the size of the slice as a percentage) are displayed:

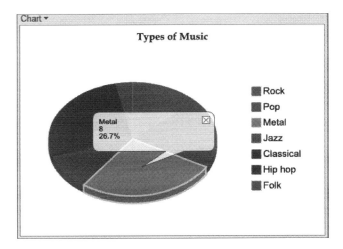

4. Click on the **Chart** drop-down menu in the top-left corner of the chart. Choose **Publish chart...**:

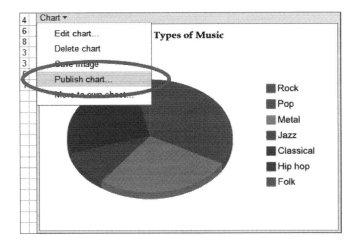

5. Right-click on the HTML code, and copy it from the Publish chart dialog.

6. Return to your Moodle course, choose a topic, make sure you have editing turned on, click on **Add a resource**, and choose **Compose a web page**.

7. To insert our pie chart, we need to copy the HTML code to Moodle's HTML editor. In the HTML editor, click on the Toggle HTML Source button:

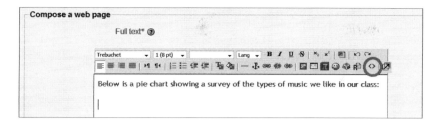

8. Cursor to the end of the HTML code in the HTML editor. Right-click and paste the HTML code we copied from Google Spreadsheets:

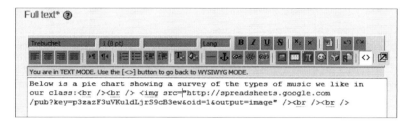

9. Click on the Toggle HTML Source button to return to WYSIWYG mode:

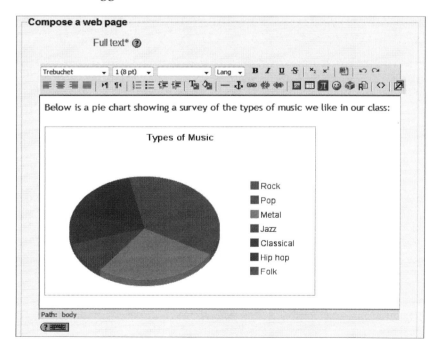

10. That's it! The pie chart is now included in our course.

Using Google Docs—recap

We've just created a pie chart in Google Spreadsheets and have seen how easy it is to insert it into a Moodle course. Check out the other types of graphs and charts you can create in Google Spreadsheets. Note that this relies on the data being (and remaining) on your Google Docs account. If you want to remove the risk of accidentally deleting the spreadsheet in Google Docs, then one option is to save the image and copy that into the course instead.

Further study—Google Chart API

We can create graphs and charts using the Google Chart API (Applications Programming Interface). Check out `http://code.google.com/apis/chart/basics.html` for more information on the API. The Google Chart API is a very powerful, advanced concept, but it's beyond the scope of this guide. However, as an example of what can be achieved, compose a web page and try copying the following code into the HTML editor (in TEXT MODE):

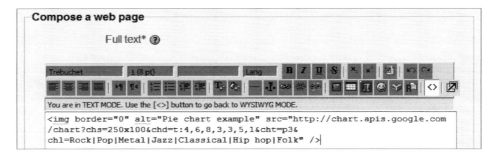

Here is what you will see when you toggle back to WYSIWYG mode:

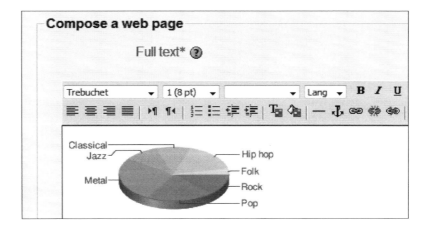

Summary

We've learned about creating, editing, and including graphs and charts in our Moodle courses. In the last chapter, we learned how to include advanced math notation into our courses using ASCIIMathML. ASCIIMathML also includes an advanced plotting function called ASCIIsvg, and we learned the basics of embedding graphs of functions into our courses using this facility. We also investigated creating graphs and charts using three spreadsheet applications: Microsoft Excel, OpenOffice. org Calc, and Google Spreadsheets. You may well have access to Excel, but if you don't, then Calc and Google Spreadsheets are both free to use.

In the next and final chapter of this book, we will be investigating examples of resources and activities for numerate disciplines in general (not just mathematics).

9
Doing More with Math and Science

We learned how to upload old mathematics exam papers to your Moodle courses (Chapter 1). We've seen that we can easily add an online discussion forum where students can discuss with teachers and their peers any problems they are having (Chapter 1). We've also learned how to include complex mathematical notation in our courses (Chapters 2 and 7) and how we can include third-party resources and activities, which are usually supplied in either SCORM or Flash format (Chapter 4). We are now able to set quizzes and tests for our students (Chapter 6) and have even looked at installing a special Moodle add-on that will recognize algebraic equivalence when checking answers (for example, $3x+4$ is equivalent to $4+3x$). We've also investigated including graphs and charts (Chapter 8) and interactive math exploration tools (specifically GeoGebra in Chapter 5).

I've already stated that incorporating mathematical notation in Moodle courses can be problematic (an issue that is being addressed in Moodle 2.0). This book is interspersed with techniques for creating the notation, from using the Word Equation Editor in Chapter 2 to the TeX filter in Chapter 7. We begin this final chapter investigating even more methods for creating mathematical (and chemical) notation.

Mathematics teachers are lucky (in a way!) in that there is a wealth of entertaining and engaging teaching resources available on the Internet for us to include in our Moodle courses. In this chapter, we will investigate how to take advantage of these resources. This chapter builds on the knowledge and experience we've gained throughout the book.

Why have I included science in this chapter? I often get asked by science teachers how they can include mathematical notation in their Moodle courses. Although this book is aimed at mathematics teachers, it can benefit teachers of any numerate discipline. One popular question from chemistry teachers is, "How can I include 3D interactive molecules in my Moodle courses?". I will provide one answer to that question at the end of this chapter. Don't worry about this problem being concerned with chemistry teaching; this problem requires us to install and use a special Moodle filter dedicated to displaying interactive molecules. It provides good practice in installing Moodle filters, which builds on experience gained in Chapter 7 where we investigated the jsMath filter. Plus, it will keep your chemistry teaching colleagues happy!

Specifically, we will learn the following:

- Alternative methods of creating mathematical (and scientific) notation
- How to include teaching resources that are available to download from the Internet
- How to install the 3D interactive molecule viewer Jmol

Alternative ways to create math notation

In this book, we have investigated the typical ways of including math notation in our Moodle courses. For example, in Chapter 7, we enabled the TeX filter and learned how to use DragMath to create the LaTeX code, which the TeX filter then converts into mathematical notation. We saw how the jsMath filter attempts to create math notation on the server but, if it fails to do so, it can attempt to do the same in the browser (in other words, the jsMath filter *degrades* gracefully).

There are still more ways to create mathematical notation using graphical user interfaces (GUIs), aside from DragMath. These alternative methods are very easy to use. Some of them rely on third-party websites to create the mathematical notation (web services). It isn't necessarily a problem until that web service is unavailable for some reason. Then, all of your nice mathematical notation will disappear!

Let's run through just a few of those tools now:

MathType

MathType is the equation editor from the authors of MathPlayer (see Chapter 7), a company called Design Science. If you've been using the Microsoft Equation Editor to create your mathematical notation, then you've been using a cut-down version of MathPlayer. MathType isn't free, but it certainly isn't expensive. Check out the Design Science website (`www.Dessci.com/MathType`) for current pricing information.

WIRIS

WIRIS is a commercial Computer Algebra System (CAS) and an equation editor (`http://www.wiris.com`). In fact, the notation editor is a small part of the complete system, which is very much like DragMath in look and feel. The advantage with WIRIS is that a Moodle plugin (the WIRIS plugin) is available that allows you to insert mathematical formulas in Moodle's HTML editor, or you can use it to insert WIRIS CAS applets. Note that WIRIS is not free.

Sitmo

Visit `http://www.sitmo.com/latex/` for a simple-to-use online equation editor. This is very similar to the equation editor included in Google Docs. However, extracting the image from the Sitmo editor is easy; simply click on it to download:

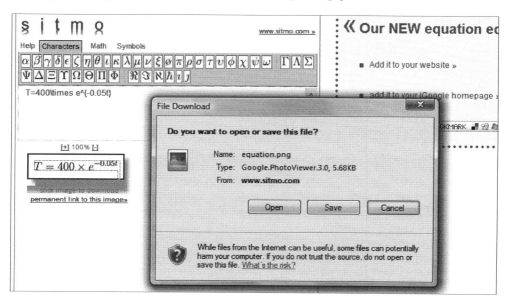

The Sitmo site provides fragments of HTML code to allow you to include the editor in your Moodle pages. This might be useful if you want your students to generate math notation.

Detexify

LaTeX is a very powerful typesetting language, but as with all powerful languages, there are times when you are stuck trying to remember a symbol. Detexify (http://detexify.kirelabs.org/classify.html#) isn't actually a mathematical notation editor: what it does is try to recognize the symbol that you draw onto a special drawing canvas, and it presents you with its LaTeX equivalent:

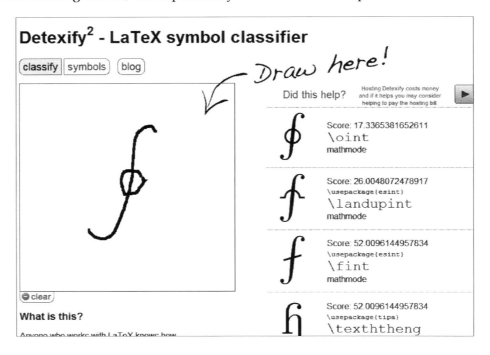

Math Input Panel (Windows 7 only)

The Math Input Panel allows you to write mathematical notation the natural way. It is designed to be used with a pen on a Tablet PC, but you can use it with any input device (including your finger on a touch screen). The notation is exported in MathML format (not that you'd notice as the Input Panel integrates seamlessly with Microsoft Word). Once you've created the notation, it can be included in your Moodle course by saving it as an image.

Math+Magic

Math+Magic is a feature-rich notation editor that is able to support LaTeX, MathML, and it is even compatible with equations generated by the Microsoft Equation Editor. This editor is not free (see `http://www.mathmagic.com` for the latest pricing information), but it is available for PCs running either the Windows or Mac operating systems.

Formulator Weaver

Formulator Weaver is a powerful, free mathematical notation editor from Hermitech Laboratory (`http://www.mmlsoft.com`). The software itself has an intuitive, easy-to-use interface:

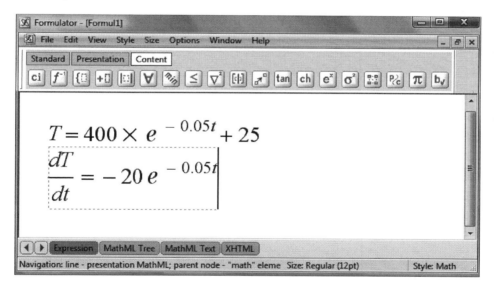

Mathematical notation can be exported as images and included in your Moodle course. However, the editor software is a Windows-only desktop client. If we wanted our students to produce mathematical notation (in a forum post, for example), then this would mean our students have to download the program to their computers in order to use it.

Google Docs and the Google Chart API

As an alternative to installing an office application suite, Google Docs provides a rudimentary equation editor:

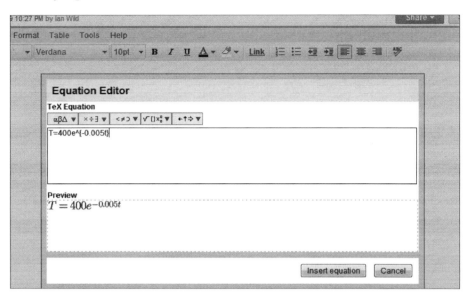

You'll need a Google account (visit `http://docs.google.com` for details). Create a new document, and select **Insert | Equation** from the main menu:

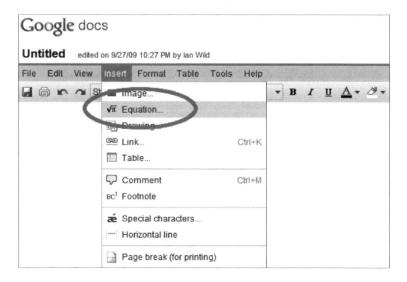

Use the Equation Editor to create a fragment of mathematical notation. The Equation Editor's preview window contains an image of the notation. You can right-click on this image and save it to your computer:

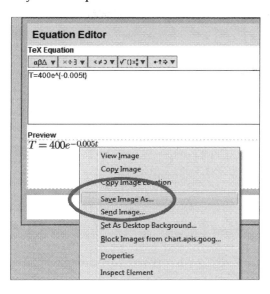

To include the notation in your Moodle course, you can add the image to your text using Moodle's HTML editor (see Chapter 2 for more details).

Recall how in Chapter 8 we used the Google Chart API to include graphs and charts in our Moodle courses? If you're feeling particularly adventurous, you can also use the Chart API to include mathematical notation:

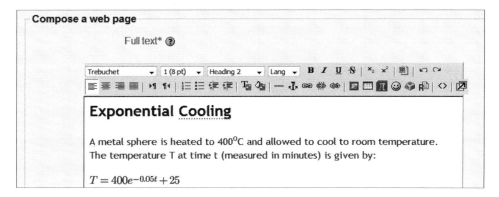

To use the Google Chart API to include mathematical notation in your Moodle course, you will need to include an image. If I switch the HTML editor to TEXT MODE, here is how I generated the mathematical notation you saw in the previous screenshot:

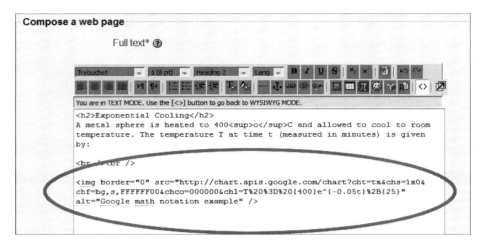

MathTran

MathTran (http://www.mathtran.org/) is a free online tool that translates LaTeX into images as a web service:

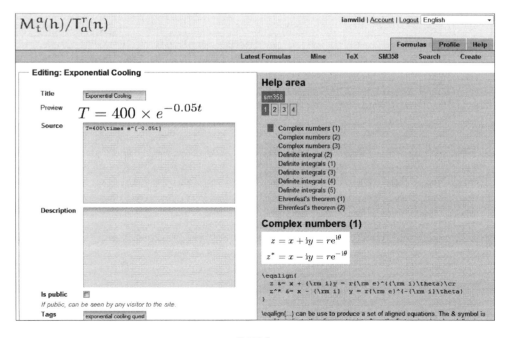

MathTran allows you to save formulas you have created, share them (for example, with colleagues), and easily include them in your Moodle course (via a web link). Recall that we can use the Google Chart API to create mathematical notation. You can do the same with MathTran. The following mathematical notation was created using MathTran:

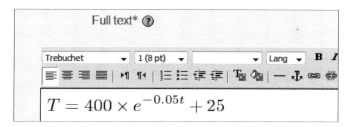

Here's the HTML code that produced it:

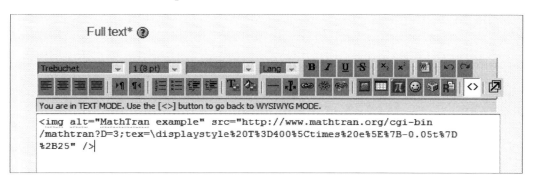

Publicon

Publicon is a specialized science notation tool from Wolfram Research (http://www.wolfram.com/products/publicon/index.html). As the name suggests, Publicon is specifically designed to support creating technical publications that include mathematical and scientific notation. Like WIRIS, MathMagic, and MathType, this tool isn't free (check out their website for the latest pricing information). Note that Publicon allows you to create chemical notation, too. There's more on chemical notation later on in this chapter.

Math teaching resources

A quick search of the Internet reveals a wealth of interactive resources you can include in your Moodle courses. One good place to start your search is Moodle.org itself. For example, `http://docs.moodle.org/en/Mathematics` lists a few examples of Java applets that can be used to support mathematics teaching (more on Java applets later in this section).

The resources you find on the Internet fall roughly into three categories:

- **Resources you can link to**: You provide a link to the resource from your Moodle course. If the person owning the resource moves it (or deletes it completely), then your link is broken and students can no longer access it.

- **Resources you can include in your Moodle course**: You upload a resource to your course, meaning you don't have to worry if someone else has moved or deleted it.

- **Resources students can download to their computer**: It doesn't matter where the resource originates because it ends up on your students' computers.

Let's look at examples of each type of resource in turn.

Resources you can link to

Enliven your Moodle course with an educational game. Fantastic Contraption (`http://fantasticcontraption.com/`) is one such game. There are two ways of providing a web link to an external resource:

- Including a **Link to a file or website** resource to your course's front page

- Converting a fragment of text into a link using the **Insert Web Link** button in the HTML editor

Recall that, in Chapter 1, we uploaded an old exam paper to the course files area and provided a link to that file on the course's front page using the **Link to a file or website** resource:

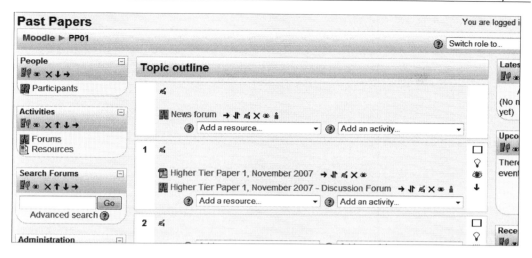

Rather than providing a link to a file in the course files area, the link we specify can just as easily be a link to any web page on the Internet. Here's how to include a link to the Fantastic Contraption game on your course's front page:

1. Return to your course's front page, and make sure editing is turned on.

2. Choose a topic and click on the **Add a resource** drop-down menu. From the list, choose **Link to a file or website**.

3. Give the new resource a name. The text you type in here is what will appear on your course's front page.

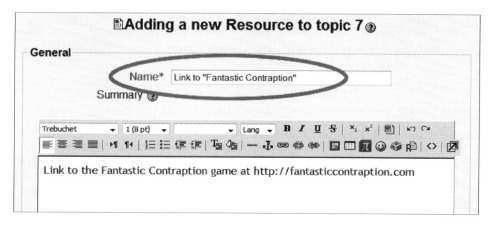

4. Scroll down to the **Window** box, and paste in the URL of the web page you want to link to:

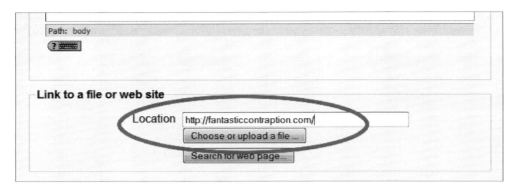

5. Click on the **Window** drop-down menu and choose **New window**:

6. Scroll down to the bottom of the page, and click on **Save and return to course** button.

7. A new resource has been added to your course's front page. If I click on mine, then the Fantastic Contraption game is displayed.

In the previous example, I specified that Moodle should display the Fantastic Contraption game in a new window. You might have valid objections for displaying Moodle resources in new windows. One is that lots of new windows can be awkward to manage on small monitors; you might not want children to have lots of windows open on their monitors if you are trying to stop them wandering around the Internet attempting to visit websites they shouldn't. If you are going to display the resource in the same window, then Moodle allows you to provide a navigation banner across the top of the page. I'm going to update my link to the Fantastic Contraption game so that Moodle displays it in the same window but with a navigation banner across the top of the page:

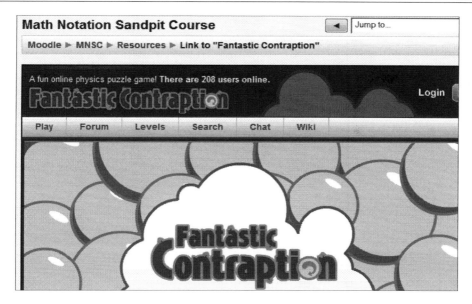

1. Return to your course's front page, and turn on the editing.

2. Find the resource you just added to your course's front page, and click on the **Update** icon next to it:

3. Scroll down to the **Window** block, and click on the **Show Advanced** button. If it has already been clicked, then you'll see a **Hide Advanced** button instead:

4. From the **Window** drop-down menu, select **Same window**. From the **Keep page navigation visible on the same page** drop-down menu, select **Yes, without frame**:

5. Scroll down to the bottom of the page, and click on the **Save and return to course** button.

6. Try clicking on the link now to see how your resource is displayed.

Most websites won't work if they are displayed inside a frame. This is because you could easily embed someone else's page inside your own by, for example, surrounding their page with lots of your own advertisements. To overcome this problem, websites try to spot whether or not they are displayed inside a frame and often fail to load if they are.

Resources you can upload

We saw in Chapter 4 how we can include SCORM and Flash format resources and activities in our Moodle courses. Another category of resources is called Java applets. There are many such applets available for math and science teaching on the Internet. So, how do we include them in our Moodle courses? Here are two options:

- We can simply link to the page containing the applet. We learned how to create links to web pages in the previous section.

- We can download the applet from the Internet, upload it to our Moodle course, and provide a link to our own copy from our course's front page.

Don't try to make unauthorized copies of copyright materials. If you are unsure, then contact the author of the website from which you are attempting to download the applet.

Here is a ripple tank simulation included in my math notation sandpit course:

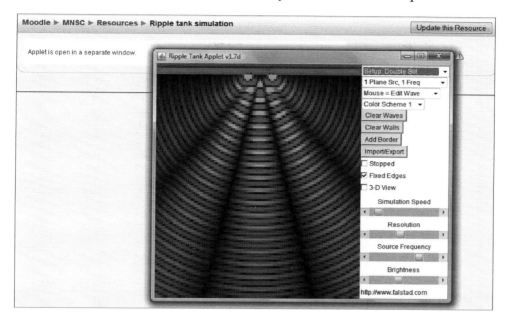

I simply downloaded the applet from Paul Falstad's excellent website at
`http://www.falstad.com/ripple/` and then uploaded it (and its associated files)
to my course files area:

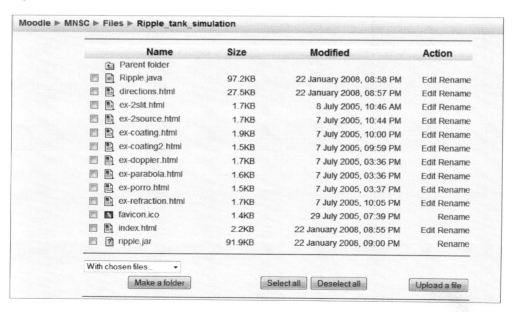

I then right-clicked on the file **ripple.jar** and copied the location of that file (note that I'm using Firefox to do this):

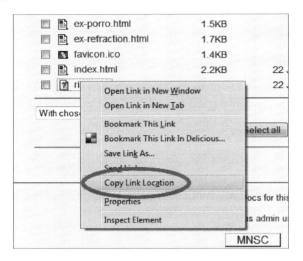

I added a new web page resource to my course's front page (through **Add a resource... | Compose a web page**), switched the HTML editor to **TEXT MODE**, and pasted in the following code (which I copied from Paul's website). I pasted the location of `ripple.jar` into the archive attribute:

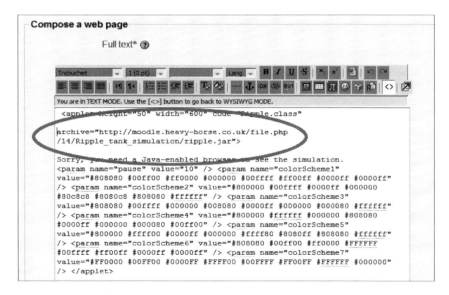

And hey presto! Students can now get access to the ripple tank simulation from my course files area.

Resources students can download

We saw in Chapter 1 (where we uploaded an old exam paper) that we can upload any digital file to Moodle. In fact, Moodle can recognize some types of files. For example, if we upload a Word document (DOC file), then Moodle will indicate the file type with a little Microsoft Word icon. But just because Moodle might not recognize all types of files doesn't mean that we can't upload it. The only caveat is that our students must have the correct software installed on their computers to allow them to view the contents.

One example is interactive whiteboard (IWB) files. I often use a SMART Board in my classroom ('SMART Board' is a brand name. Another popular brand is ActivBoard from Promethean). If I have created a SMART Notebook file to use in my face-to-face teaching, I can easily upload that file to my Moodle course to allow students to explore the file at their leisure. However, my students must have the relevant software installed on their computer if they are going to be able to open the file correctly. To overcome that problem, I provide a link to a special student edition of the SMART Notebook software and a warning that they will have to install this software before they are able to view the contents of the file.

Science modules

The reason I wanted to include a short section on science teaching in a mathematics book is that I often get asked about mathematical notation by science teachers, which is understandable, but I also get asked about chemical symbols, too:

The Haber Process

Fritz Haber and his specia ammonia is the basis for t nitrogen fertilizer that is pr because of Fritz Haber's v food we need to feed ours

There were lots of technic order to make ammonia (r pressure) and we'll be lea course. Fritz Haber eventu his work.

Below is the chemical equation that you will need t

$$N_{2(g)} + H_{2(g)} \rightleftharpoons NH_{3(g)}$$

Notice the reversible reaction symbol (right and left the reaction can go either way.

For example, included in the following screenshot is the LaTeX code needed to produce the chemical equation for the Haber Process:

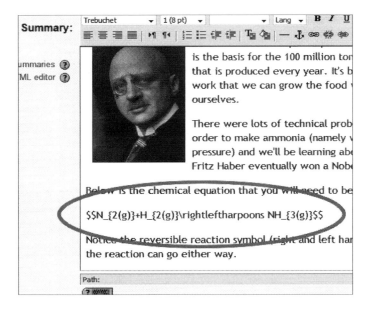

Note that not all LaTeX interpreters can support the more general typesetting notation like the reversible reaction symbol.

I also get asked about representing chemical structures in Moodle courses. A great free tool is Jmol (http://www.jmol.org/). Jmol is an open source Java viewer for chemical structures in 3D. The molecules themselves are described in special files (with the extension .pdb) that are freely available to download from the Internet. For example, a good source of these special files for simple molecules is http://qsad.bu.edu/data/pdbfiles/, provided by the Quantum Science Across Disciplines (QSAD) Project:

Index of /data/pdbfiles

```
Icon  Name                           Last modified      Size  Description

[DIR] Parent Directory                                    -
[   ] (E)-Hex-3-ene.pdb              19-Sep-2001 12:28  1.3K
[   ] (Z)-Hex-3-ene.pdb              19-Sep-2001 12:28  1.3K
[   ] 123-Trichlorobenzene..>        19-Sep-2001 12:28  922
[   ] 1crn.pdb                       19-Sep-2001 12:28   34K
[   ] 2-Methylbicyclo[2.1...>        19-Sep-2001 12:28  1.2K
[   ] 2-Methylpropane.pdb            19-Sep-2001 12:28  1.0K
[   ] 2-amino-2-deoxy-D-gl..>        19-Sep-2001 12:28  1.8K
[   ] 22 dichloro-111 trif..>        19-Sep-2001 12:28  662
[   ] 22me3ane.pdb                   19-Sep-2001 12:28  1.2K
[   ] 22me4ane.pdb                   19-Sep-2001 12:28  1.4K
[   ] 23me4ane.pdb                   19-Sep-2001 12:28  1.4K
[   ] 2me-4ane.pdb                   19-Sep-2001 12:28  1.2K
[   ] 2me-5ane.pdb                   19-Sep-2001 12:28  1.4K
[   ] 3cro.pdb                       19-Sep-2001 12:28  161K
[   ] 3me-5ane.pdb                   19-Sep-2001 12:28  1.4K
[   ] 6-deoxy-D-glucose.pdb          19-Sep-2001 12:28  1.7K
[   ] A.pdb                          19-Sep-2001 12:28  2.6K
[   ] Aniline.pdb                    19-Sep-2001 12:28  1.0K
```

Here is an example of an ammonia molecule displayed in Moodle using the Jmol viewer:

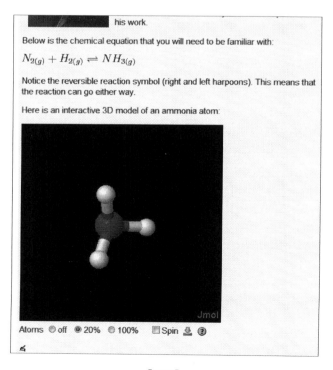

Students can manipulate the molecule in three dimensions and zoom in and out. What's great about online modeling is that I no longer have to worry about losing all my little plastic atoms. Carbon atoms seemed to be the ones that always went missing, apparently because they could be fired from an elastic band more easily.

For example, imagine I'm trying to describe the difference in the molecular structures of graphite and diamond. Including 3D representations of those molecules in Moodle makes that task easy, and it allows the students to explore those molecules independently (without firing plastic atoms at each other or out of the window).

How do we incorporate Jmol into Moodle? You'll need FTP access to your server. I'm going to be using FileZilla running on a Windows PC (the process is the same using different FTP tools on different operating systems). Let's learn how to install Jmol now:

1. Download the Jmol filter from the Moodle.org website (`http://moodle.org/mod/data/view.php?d=13&rid=88&filter=1`).

2. Unzip the file, and copy the contents into the filter directory in your Moodle installation using your FTP client:

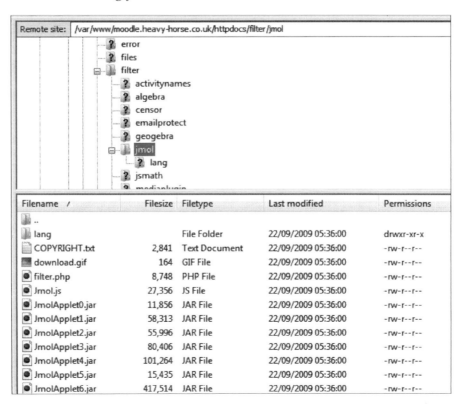

3. Look inside the **jmol** folder, and you'll find a folder called **lang**. Look inside this and you will see a set of folders containing help files for Jmol in different languages. My installation is using the en_utf8 language pack, so I need to look inside the en_utf8/help folder and copy the subfolder called jmol into the lang/en_utf8/help folder inside my Moodle installation on the server:

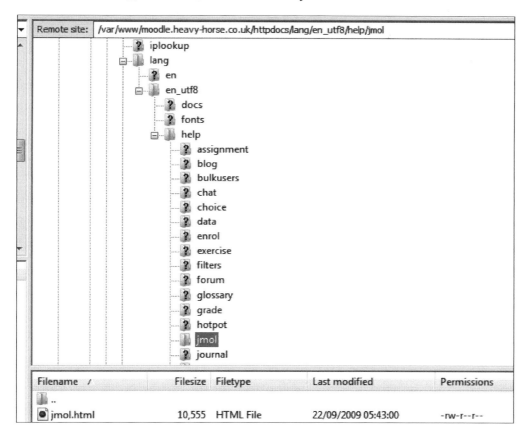

4. You will now need to log into Moodle using an admin account. In the **Site Administration** block, select **Modules | Filters | Manage filters**:

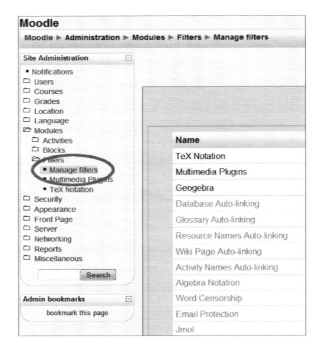

5. Look for **Jmol** in the list of filters, and poke the eye to enable it:

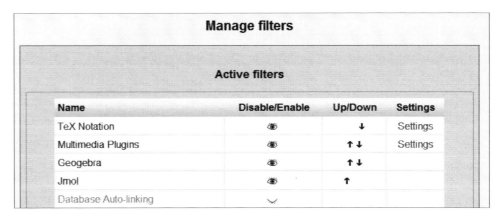

6. That's it! We are now ready to start including interactive 3D molecules in our Moodle courses.

Let's now test the filter. A sample PDB file (called `manywater.pdb`) is included inside the Jmol package we downloaded from Moodle.org. Follow these steps:

1. Open a Moodle course.
2. Upload the sample file to the course files area.
3. Turn on the editing, choose a topic, and select **Compose a web page** from the **Add a resource** drop-down menu.
4. Enter some text.
5. Turn the text into a web link to the PDB file in your course files area.

Your text link will be replaced by the Jmol viewer:

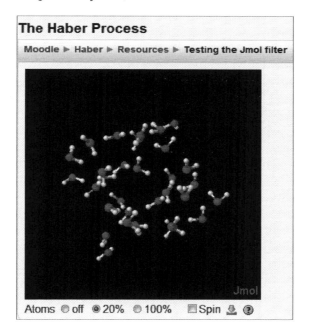

 Right-click on a molecule and choose Render | Stereographic from the menu. There you will find options to display molecules in 3D suitable for viewing using 3D glasses (for example, red-cyan glasses). You'll find the glasses you need very cheap to purchase on the Internet.

Summary

We began this chapter by completing our investigation of methods of incorporating mathematical notation in our Moodle courses. These methods often rely on third-party services to render the notation. That's fine until those services fail; then your course, without its notation, may become unusable.

A quick search of the Internet finds a wealth of resources for mathematics teaching. We investigated various ways of incorporating these resources in our Moodle courses.

I have also included a discussion of a 3D interactive molecule viewer in this chapter. Why? Because I often get asked by science teachers how they can include mathematical notation in their Moodle courses, and I wanted to recognize that it's likely that you might not be a mathematics teacher. Also, the tool I describe (Jmol) requires us to install a special Moodle filter (building on experience gained in Chapter 7, where we investigated the jsMath filter).

Remember, if you need more advice and guidance on teaching mathematics with Moodle, then join me and my colleagues in the Moodle.org Mathematics Tools forum at http://moodle.org/mod/forum/view.php?id=752.

Index

Thank you for buying
Moodle 1.9 Math

Packt Open Source Project Royalties

When we sell a book written on an Open Source project, we pay a royalty directly to that project. Therefore by purchasing Moodle 1.9 Math, Packt will have given some of the money received to the Moodle project.

In the long term, we see ourselves and you — customers and readers of our books — as part of the Open Source ecosystem, providing sustainable revenue for the projects we publish on. Our aim at Packt is to establish publishing royalties as an essential part of the service and support a business model that sustains Open Source.

If you're working with an Open Source project that you would like us to publish on, and subsequently pay royalties to, please get in touch with us.

Writing for Packt

We welcome all inquiries from people who are interested in authoring. Book proposals should be sent to author@packtpub.com. If your book idea is still at an early stage and you would like to discuss it first before writing a formal book proposal, contact us; one of our commissioning editors will get in touch with you.

We're not just looking for published authors; if you have strong technical skills but no writing experience, our experienced editors can help you develop a writing career, or simply get some additional reward for your expertise.

About Packt Publishing

Packt, pronounced 'packed', published its first book "Mastering phpMyAdmin for Effective MySQL Management" in April 2004 and subsequently continued to specialize in publishing highly focused books on specific technologies and solutions.

Our books and publications share the experiences of your fellow IT professionals in adapting and customizing today's systems, applications, and frameworks. Our solution-based books give you the knowledge and power to customize the software and technologies you're using to get the job done. Packt books are more specific and less general than the IT books you have seen in the past. Our unique business model allows us to bring you more focused information, giving you more of what you need to know, and less of what you don't.

Packt is a modern, yet unique publishing company, which focuses on producing quality, cutting-edge books for communities of developers, administrators, and newbies alike. For more information, please visit our website: www.PacktPub.com.

Moodle 1.9 for Second Language Teaching

ISBN: 978-1-847196-24-8   Paperback: 524 pages

Engaging online language learning activities using the Moodle platform

1. A recipe book for creating language activities using Moodle 1.9

2. Get the most out of Moodle 1.9's features to create enjoyable, useful language learning activities

3. Create an online language learning center that includes reading, writing, speaking, listening, vocabulary, and grammar activities

Moodle 1.9 Multimedia

ISBN: 978-1-847195-90-6   Paperback: 272 pages

Create and share multimedia learning materials in your Moodle courses.

1. Ideas and best practices for teachers and trainers on using multimedia effectively in Moodle

2. Ample screenshots and clear explanations to facilitate learning

3. Covers working with TeacherTube, embedding interactive Flash games, podcasting, and more

4. Create instructional materials and design students' activities around multimedia

Please check **www.PacktPub.com** for information on our titles

Made in the USA
Lexington, KY
24 April 2010